BETTER NEXT YEAR

An Anthology of Christmas Epiphanies

BETTER
NEXT
YEAR

EDITED BY JJ LEE

Published by Tidewater Press
New Westminster, BC, Canada
tidewaterpress.ca

978-1-990160-27-1 (print)
978-1-990160-28-8 (e-book)

"The Harlequin Set" by JJ Lee first published online by
Montecristo Magazine, December 21, 2022.

LIBRARY AND ARCHIVES CANADA CATALOGUING IN PUBLICATION
Title: Better next year : an anthology of Christmas epiphanies / edited by JJ Lee.
Names: Lee, J. J. (James-Jason), editor.
Identifiers: Canadiana (print) 20230545734 | Canadiana (ebook) 20230545742 | ISBN 9781990160271
(softcover) | ISBN 9781990160288 (EPUB)
Subjects: LCSH: Christmas—Psychological aspects—Anecdotes. | LCSH: Christmas—Canada—Anecdotes. |
LCSH: Holiday stress—Anecdotes. | LCSH: Minority authors—Canada—Anecdotes. | CSH: Authors,
Canadian (English)—Anecdotes. | LCGFT: Anecdotes.

Classification: LCC GT4987.15 .B48 2023 | DDC 394.26630971—dc23

**TIDEWATER
PRESS**

Printed in Canada

Contents

To Aunt Linda, from whom I received the gift of socks and underwear, which, by the way, are the only items I now want for Christmas.

EDITOR'S NOTE

JJ LEE

About five years ago, with no real reason or instigation, people started sharing with me personal stories of absolutely horrible Christmases. I remember one writer, known both for her memoir and fiction, who recounted an abysmal holiday season involving homelessness, soup-kitchen turkey dinners, and lice, all the while being feted as a rising literary star. This may say too much about me, but I laughed, and maybe even hooted, with every sad twist of the tale.

It was just so horrible and beautiful. Though I'm not Christian nor religious in any way, it reminded me how many times in my life I had pinned outsized expectations of joy and happiness on those final seven days of the year only to be met by disappointment, if not sheer disaster. Over the winter holidays, every plan we make, action we take, and outcome that falls upon us is magnified. Possibly by then the year is so long and old that we enter those final weeks with our nerves raw and frayed, so we feel it all.

I became a collector of these woeful true-life tales set in call centres, shelters, and rehabs with writers finding themselves totally broke, or away from home, alone or stuck with near-strangers, or worse, hostile future in-laws. And three questions kept popping up in my mind: "Why am I laughing?" "Could this be an anthology?" and "What is up with writers?"

The answer to the first question is I was always astonished and delighted by the lengths to which the storytellers held onto hope and sought out peace, joy, and happiness, in any amounts they could obtain. The answer to the second is in your hands. And the final one, well, I leave that to you to determine. But it's possible that writers are no different from anyone else. Enjoy.

And Happy Holidays.

Tortues de Noël

SONJA LARSEN

The room came with a turtle. Jean-Pierre didn't know how long the turtle had been in the basement, but it was there when he moved in. It was very easy to care for. I'd have the whole basement to myself—a main room with the large built-in aquarium, as well as a little bedroom. My ex-husband and I had turtles too, which seemed like a weird coincidence. I said I'd take it. The rent was cheap. Maybe too cheap. Was it the turtle or did he think having an Anglo girl, a waitress, in the apartment would bring in other girls? He soon found out I only brought home friends for sleepovers. Some stayed friends, but most were just fresh grief, fresh distraction from my recent breakup.

My new roommate was never going to be a friend or a distraction. He was stocky and pale and his father paid the rent for him. He seemed like a toddler who didn't know his own strength. There was no chance of things getting blurry, which was a relief. Too many things already felt blurry. We didn't have a lot in common but I didn't mind making small talk, an opportunity for a free, if slightly dull, language exchange. The turtle. *La tortue.* The weather. A lot of life advice he'd gotten from his dad. His

3

dad was a prison psychiatrist who believed in working hard and being realistic. Being realistic was what made Jean-Pierre drop out of med school and study pharmacology instead. There's no shame in that, he said, like I'd implied there might be. I was studying liberal arts so who was I to judge? His pharmacology studies didn't seem limited to school. Over time I realized Jean-Pierre had drugs for studying or partying, calming down or perking up. Some days he was scrubbing the bathtub with a toothbrush and other days he could hardly get out of bed.

Pills weren't really my thing. Once, when I was nervous for a test, he gave me something but I got too stoned to even focus on the page. Not that I was against drugs. I liked pot and hash, cocaine maybe a little too much. I liked my vices to hit me right away. I didn't want surprises. It shouldn't have been a surprise to find myself getting divorced at twenty-three and yet it was. Like a post you walk into when you're drunk, you step back and wonder how you ever managed not to see it.

I'd stormed out of our place after I found out my husband was cheating on me. He couldn't leave me if I left him first. He kept the apartment, the aquarium with our two turtles, while I'd moved into a series of temporary living arrangements, a friend's couch, my dad's guest room, until I'd landed in this basement room. And instead of living my forever life, I woke up every day surprised to find myself in a basement on

Saint Dominique Street with an abandoned reptile and a pill-popping boy.

For a guy with access to a lot of drugs, Jean-Pierre didn't seem to have many friends to share them with. Maybe he had friends, and I just missed them. I was at school or sleeping most days and out most nights. I was a waitress and a regular at a few bars on The Main—the Balmoral, the Bifteque, Bar Saint-Laurent, Double Deuce, Café de Poet. I was heartbroken and lonely but seldom alone. Still, it never occurred to me that Jean-Pierre was sad too until a week before Christmas when he almost jumped off the Champlain Bridge.

I heard about the shutdown, but it wasn't until the next morning when his dad showed up and let himself in with the key that I learned it was Jean-Pierre. His dad had brought moving boxes. There had been an incident. His son was in the hospital. When he got out of the hospital, he was moving back home. With his crisp haircut and clenched jaw, he looked like a man used to institutions, used to being obeyed. I've got a month, the dad tells me. Then he's going to break the lease. I kept waiting for him to ask me about Jean-Pierre, maybe the pills, maybe if he's been different lately. But the only questions the doctor asked were about kitchen items—whose cup was this? Whose pan? Maybe he thought this obviously hungover Anglo woman didn't have the answers, or maybe he just didn't want to know.

Joyeux Noël, I said as he was leaving and I don't know if I meant it to be sarcastic or polite. Of course he was not going to have a joyous Christmas.

Joyeux Noël. I was probably five and just starting school, the first in my family to begin learning French. We'd only recently moved to Quebec. My parents had begun asking me how to say things—What is this called? How do you say that? I had questions too. Was *Père Noël* like Santa? Yes. Was Santa real? No, my mother told me. He was a lie people told to trick children into being good. And God, the *Bon Dieu*? Also a lie. But when I spread that truth to the neighbourhood kids, they weren't allowed to play with me anymore. Hippy American heathens.

After we'd been in Quebec a few years, my parents decided to check out a commune in California. My fifteen-year-old sister chose staying alone in Montreal over moving to a farm full of grownups and no boundaries, but eight-year-old me had to go. My first Christmas on the commune, we used the $25 my grandparents sent me to buy gas for the communal backhoe. I got a lamb I was supposed to raise as food.

Sometimes my sister and I play the 'who had the worst childhood game,' and we're always convinced that the other one is winning.

At the commune, people were always coming and going but after a while they mostly go. We lasted a year, maybe a bit more. No one knew how to farm, or even get along. The commune was over, and so was my parents' marriage. My dad moved back to Montreal. My mother and I stayed on at the commune as long as we could but eventually we left too, moving into a nearby small town. My sister moved nearby but lived on her own even though she was only seventeen.

After the commune broke up, our family began the only real holiday tradition we ever had—the tearful long-distance phone call. Which parent I lived with and how long I stayed changed from year to year. Every phone call was a negotiation. Even when it was just the smallest things—the time difference, who was going to pay for the call, how long I could stay on the line—the phone calls were hard. *Did it get there on time?* The present that cost as much to send as it was worth. *Did you like it? I don't know what you like now.*

When I was sixteen, what I liked, what I wanted, all changed in one summer. My dad married his girlfriend. A friend died in a suicide pact. Suddenly I didn't want red shoes or a new jacket, the latest album. I wanted justice, meaning, a place where I knew I was wanted. And conveniently enough, I knew just the place.

To be fair, my mother didn't know the organization she spent years working for was a cult. No one ever does. She'd spent her time in a community office in Northern California where she'd been a welfare advocate, a community leader, running a food bank and more. She was a full-time unpaid volunteer for an organization that she believed was going to change the world. But even on the days when it was hard to believe in the promise of an imminent proletarian revolution, she could still feel good about the work she did.

As a young teen, I'd helped out when I'd lived with her: gone on soup lines, handed out leaflets, made decorations for the free Christmas dinner. I thought I'd be doing the same kinds of work when I decided to spend the summer with the group's east coast wing. Instead I ended up at the organization's national headquarters, a few brownstone apartments in a Brooklyn neighbourhood decades away from gentrification. Ninety of us lived and worked there, coordinating the efforts of the field offices, recruiting new members into the Party, soliciting donations, and most of all, answering when our leader called.

You'd think Christmas in a cult might be bleak, but actually, it could be one of the happiest times of year in our safehouse. One difference between a commune and a cult is that things are much more organized in a cult. At Christmas time, the donors to our front charities were generous, and there was never any argument about who was going to cook, who was going to clean. It was also one of the only times of the year we got to drink. My first year, there was a poker game and I won and lost $60, all in pennies. I didn't need much—a little whiskey, penny-ante poker, the promise of a better tomorrow—to be happy.

*

But after that promise was gone, and I lost faith in the leader and the deadlines he kept setting and missing, there was not enough whiskey or pennies to make me want to stay. Although by then it was a lot harder to leave. Because that's another difference between a commune and a cult. In a commune people come and go, but in a cult there is no going. I'd seen the bruises on those who tried.

But I did get out, celebrating my nineteenth birthday by stealing spare change and sprinting out the back door at dawn. I made it to the subway, made it to a Western Union, and eventually back to Montreal, and my old/new life. For months, all I wanted to do was cry and get high and dance. On the dance floor I could grieve or celebrate being free, and I didn't even have to choose. I didn't need a manifesto, a leader, a movement. All I needed to do was find the beat.

Dancing to Bauhaus was how I met my husband. He said nobody else ever danced to that song. I'll dance to almost anything, I told him. Within months we were living together, and I was planning a wedding. It started out as a way to get more student loans and just in case I had immigration troubles from all the hippy record-keeping and moving back and forth. But it turned into fifty guests and purple and silver balloons, and a lesbian Unitarian minister quoting James Baldwin. We held the wedding at my father's house and my stepmother made the appetizers, baked the wedding cake. The cake was beautiful, but the wedding was

BETTER NEXT YEAR

*

a disaster. A great-uncle made lecherous remarks, my husband's brother had a psychotic break in the garden. My new husband cried, and not from joy.

My husband and I only had one holiday tradition. We didn't hang a tree or decorations. We were students and always broke. We had difficult families and weren't even sure we believed in celebrating Christmas. But we always bought something special, something unnecessary as a gift to ourselves. That must have been how we got the turtles. The little red-eared slider and a more exotic box turtle that liked to bite. Even in the midst of all of our drama, there was still something peaceful about their relentless green existence.

More money for school, sex on a regular basis, reptiles, and a distraction from sadness. That was all my husband wanted. He wanted things that were simple, honest, dependable. But after a few years of marriage, I was turning out to be none of those things. Instead of the opinionated and sexually adventurous woman he'd taken home one night, someone else had taken her place. A woman coming down off the adrenaline of escape, a woman who thought too much, studied too much, cried too much. Maybe I didn't really blame him for wanting someone else.

Christmas on Saint Laurent Boulevard was a mixed bag of merry and maudlin. I wasn't a particularly good waitress, but one job led to another, and I worked at a few different places. At the Bifteque, a lot of the students went home for the holidays. Sometimes you didn't know a regular was rich until they disappeared for three weeks and came back with a tan. At Bar Saint Laurent, the crowd was a little older and while most were broke from shopping, some were generous. A large tip, a shot of tequila, a joint, a quarter of cocaine folded into a tiny silver package. An old man tipped me $20 for his beer and told me I reminded him of his dead wife. Then he pulled me close and tried to stuff his tongue in my mouth. When I pushed him away he cried, "I'm so lonely. I'm just so lonely." And part of me felt sorry for him but the other part could still taste his Molson-flavoured spit.

When I told the other waitress what happened, she was horrified. Working in bars was the first time I'd experienced the solidarity of women. In the cult, we'd been encouraged not to gossip, especially about our leader. Could someone have warned me? Would I have listened? Me and the other waitresses on The Main exchanged information about everything. The men we were interested in, the men we should watch out for. The lousy tippers and men who tried to grab our asses. "So he's lonely," she said. "That's not your fucking problem."

It felt like my problem. It had always felt like my problem. Christmas money for gasoline, the meat for the table. All the days I spent in Brooklyn thinking I was working for something better. My husband crying in the garden. Jean-Pierre on the bridge. The loneliness of strangers, their hands around my wrist. Whose problems were they if not mine?

On Christmas Eve, I took the métro and the 103 to my dad's house through the powdery white streets of NDG, each stop a memory. Here was where the tailor was, the shoemaker, the place that sold the donuts I bought after school.

Some people say that home is the place you can always go back to, and others that home is the place you can never return to again. My dad and stepmother's two-storey house felt like something in between. I'd only lived here for three years, from thirteen to sixteen, but it was the longest I'd ever lived in one house. I'd returned briefly after the cult, and again after the breakup, a pattern I could see alarmed my stepmother. I called her that, but really she was only twelve years older than I was. Their young son had my old room so I'd stayed in the guest room. Maybe my dad said, "Stay as long as you need," but we both would have known that wasn't really true.

Opening family presents on Christmas Eve and eating catered tea sandwiches with the crusts cut off was the tradition in my stepmother's family. It had started with staying up for midnight Mass but it also gave the children toys to play with in the morning so their parents could sleep in until it was time to open the presents from Santa. Her family was loud and large and had been nothing but kind to me ever since I came into their lives as a young teenager. I filled up on ham and pimento cheese sandwiches, drank as fast as I could, and made awkward small talk about school. I studied things with complicated names like Intro to Gender Ideology in Post-war American Cinema. When people asked what kind of work you could get with that, I didn't even pretend to have an answer.

As we ate, we opened the presents. I think I got a pink flannel bathrobe and bubble bath. I remembered thinking they were the sort of gifts you might give an invalid or a teenager. And then, when we were all done, before we'd even cleaned up all the torn wrapping paper, my father offered to drive me home. What did I expect? An invitation to stay? A present from Santa? That they would just let me ride it out for a few days? Let me curl up in my flannel gown on their couch? Like a teenager, like an invalid.

"Sure," I said, "that would be great."

I don't know what we talked about on the ride home. Somewhere along the line, I had become someone my dad was a little afraid of. My mother's daughter. Joining her cult, marrying young, those things didn't help, but it started even before that. Maybe it would have been different if they'd stayed together. Not that he didn't love me. But maybe he would have loved me more. I remember that first winter we all moved to Quebec, how he took me out in the snow and taught me to make snow angels. Stretching our arms to make the biggest wings.

Once I was back in my empty apartment, the frozen composure that had gotten me through the ride home fell apart completely. I was already crying too hard to go out anywhere, too sad even for a bar full of strangers, even for a phone call to my sister or mother. It was not even nine o'clock on Christmas Eve and I had half a bottle of white wine and a pack of cigarettes to get me through. I wasn't ready for my first Christmas alone. What had I been thinking? Why hadn't I planned, hoarded the small gifts of drugs I'd been offered? Maybe I'd been trying not to think about it at all.

I walked through the apartment, to Jean-Pierre's room. Empty. I looked in the medicine cabinet. Empty. I could hear the sound of my own crying in my ears, frantic, child-like. I wasn't ready for this. I didn't know how to be ready for this. I went back to Jean-Pierre's room, looked under his bed, through his drawers. Nothing. I pushed his mattress off the bed, as much in rage as in hope, and a small brown envelope fell onto the floor. I tried not to be optimistic. His dad worked for a prison, he'd have found it already, taken whatever was inside. It was going to be empty. It was definitely going to be empty.

But it was not empty.

Inside were four blue pills.

*

I took the first pill and washed it down with some wine. I didn't care what it did so long as it made me feel different. In its murky tank, the turtle stared at me, eyes half in and out of the water. The TV only got a few stations but one of them was playing *It's a Wonderful Life*, colourized so everything looked real and fake at the same time. Zuzu with her broken flower. George standing on the bridge. The snow falling. Everything began to feel floaty and far away, like I was someone else watching that young woman in her basement room. Yet another room she was going to have to leave. But I could see what would stay with me for a long time: that although she was young and lost, lonely and maybe a little broken, that girl in the pink robe was smart enough to know a Christmas miracle when it came her way.

B v. J

WILEY WEI-CHIUN HO

Though neither of us would admit it, things were getting serious—in a good way. Sam and I couldn't see enough of each other, so I took him home to meet Lucas, my ten-year-old. I watched, relieved, then amazed at how quickly they took to each other. After supper, Sam accepted one cup of green tea which flowed into three, snuggling with me and Lucas on the couch for an episode of *Modern Family*, before the bedtime protest from Lucas: "Please, just ten more minutes!"

It didn't take long for the three of us to feel like a unit, like Sam had always been a part of the family. After years of single parenting and a disastrous relationship, the ease felt like a gift. Yes, things were good, but Sam and I agreed to take it slow.

As summer ebbed into winter, it grew harder to say goodnight before Sam headed out into the rain-soaked streets of North Vancouver, back to his apartment. We were keeping up the ruse of separate households, even as the small cups of tea became deep mugs of cocoa and Sam's cat naps on the couch lengthened to sleepovers. We were pretending we were still just dating, not so much for my son's sake as for Sam's parents'. They were born-again Christians who would not take well to our living together out of wedlock.

"They are pretty righteous," Sam warned. "They make Jehovah's Witnesses seem passive."

One night at dinner, Lucas asked Sam, "Are your parents funny like you? When do we get to meet them?"

Sam's face stiffened slightly, matching my own nervousness. I laughed and said to Lucas that he was confused about how heredity works, that children take after parents, not the other way around. But Lucas wasn't sidetracked by my clumsy diversion.

"Don't your parents want to meet us too?"

"Lucas, that's not up to you." I widened my eyes at my son, who mimicked my raised eyebrows and mirrored my expression.

"Mom, you're always asking about my friends' parents. I'm just asking too."

The kid had a point, of course. But I wasn't ready to meet Sam's parents. From what Sam said, I might not ever be ready to meet them.

When Sam left the faith in his thirties, his parents banned him from their house until he returned to the Lord. They called him day and night, alternating between begging and haranguing before finally hanging up. This went on for a year until Sam reminded them about their own faith: "Don't you believe that God works in mysterious ways?"

I studied Sam, who was studying the vegetables on his plate like they held a hidden message. I needed him to weigh in. They were his parents.

Sam glanced up with a bleak smile. "Maybe you can meet them at Christmas. That's only a month away."

"That's forever!" Lucas protested. Like a hound on a scent, he sniffed that something was up.

An only child raised by a working mom, my son was preternaturally mature, people told me, but I worried he was just adulted. Lucas was protective of me, especially after my divorce from his father, who moved to Hong Kong as soon as the papers were signed. Lucas had sensed that Sam was a keeper before I did. The first time Sam was over, Lucas dragged him into his room to show him a world map on the wall with red pushpins in places we'd been. He even poured out his precious tub of LEGO and invited Sam to build worlds with him. After Sam left, Lucas wheedled me for information. Does Sam like camping? Does he have a bike? Is Sam your boyfriend?

At the table, Lucas piped up again, his eyes shining. "I know, let's invite them over here."

A week later, our doorbell rang on the dot of six.

I had just finished lining up our usual jumble of shoes by the front door into a tidy row. Like a receiving line of footwear, I'd carefully positioned the shoes in ascending order: Lucas's mud-stained runners beside my low heels next to Sam's size-12 loafers.

It would have been easier to stash the shoes in a closet, but no. Sam and I had decided it was time to dispense with the pretenses and be open about our relationship. I wanted the evidence of our combined lives out in plain view, a declaration without my having to say a word. It was a chickenshit move, but sometimes the chicken just needs to cross the road.

I rushed to open the door with Lucas beside me. Sucking in a big breath, I swung open the door to Sam's now familiar six-one frame. Standing beside him, a stately looking couple, tall with matching grey hair, square glasses, wide smiles. Sam stepped forward to make the introductions.

"Mom and Dad, this is my wonderful girlfriend." He leaned in to give me a quick kiss, then high-fived Lucas. "And here is my main man."

"Welcome to our house," Lucas boomed beside me. His face flushed as he repeated what I'd instructed him to say earlier that day, "May I take your coats?" Lucas reached up both his arms to our guests, charming them instantly.

The parents stepped into the foyer and stopped. Their

gaze travelled over the line of shoes—small, medium, large—to their son who still had his boots on, back to the large loafers in the lineup. For a second there was only the sound of Lucas rummaging in the closet for empty hangers.

Sam's mother was the first to regain her composure. She raised her eyes to meet mine, forcing her mouth into a smile. "What a lovely house."

"Yes, thank you for the dinner invitation," Sam's father chimed in. "Something smells good."

Sam's parents were eager to move on, but I wasn't ready yet. I'd gone to some trouble, agonizing over the shoes. I wanted them to notice. I didn't want to have to pretend around Lucas or tiptoe around the proverbial elephant all night.

"We don't wear outside shoes inside," I blurted. "It's an Asian thing, sorry."

Why was I apologizing? Why weren't they saying anything? I looked at Sam, but he only shrugged.

Sam's parents slipped off their shoes and made off into the living room like passengers about to miss the last train. Lucas returned from coat-hanging duty and offered to take them on a tour of the house. They went from room to room, Sam's parents punctiliously ignoring Sam's shirts draped over chairs, Sam's shaving kit in the bathroom, three toothbrushes in a cozy cup by the sink. They only noted the lovely hardwood floors, the nice big windows. It wasn't until they entered my kitchen that all hell broke loose.

Sam's mother gasped. She took one look at the large Buddha on the shelf above the stove and whirled around. She clutched her husband's arm as if she feared losing consciousness. Under her breath, she whispered a prayer fast and low, maybe an exorcism. Sam's father hung onto her, the two of them clinging tight like the floor might suddenly open up and swallow them whole.

Then Sam's father took charge. He straightened up and stood taller. Deliberately, he looked at the Buddha and then at the dining room table across from the kitchen. His gaze swung back and forth like he was measuring the path of an asteroid. Finally, he cleared his throat and spoke.

"I'm afraid *that*," his head inclined toward Buddha, "will have to be moved or we cannot eat at the table."

I knew they were devout but this was ludicrous. Smiling Buddha. Really?

"You can face away from the kitchen," I said, keeping my voice light. I pointed to the seats looking out to the patio, away from the offending statue.

I started to ramble into the silence, explaining how I had inherited the carving from my parents when they moved back to Taiwan. It's mahogany, I said, very old. It had belonged to my paternal grandparents. In their house, where three generations of my family used to live, the statue had a special place in the living room. On an altar made of jade, Buddha presided over our home with his chubby cheerfulness. If my cousins and I chased each other into the living room when there were guests, we'd get in trouble with the grownups. But Buddha never minded. He'd just keep on radiating his generous smile like he'd just learned something delightful.

"You see, my grandparents were the faithful Buddhists. They used to go to temple all the time, whereas I'm more of a Buddhist in principle. I'm a terrible vegetarian and I always slap mosquitoes."

Sam and Lucas laughed but Sam's parents were stone-faced.

I babbled some more, trying to lighten the mood. I knew I was overcompensating. I sounded like my parents when they first came to this country, over-explaining and apologizing for being different, trying to make people comfortable so they wouldn't view us as a threat.

Sam's parents refused to budge.

"We will not be in the presence of a false idol," Sam's father said, his voice clear and solemn. "There is only one God and He is Jesus Christ, our Lord and Savior." He turned to Sam. "I'm shocked at you, son. They don't know better, but you do."

"Dad, we've been through this." Sam looked imploringly at his mother but she said nothing. She stood quietly beside her husband, her body language affirming what her husband said, what the Good Book instructed: Follow your husband as he follows Christ.

"God is love," Sam's father continued. "You mustn't turn away."

"Actually," I said, my face flushing, "Buddhism teaches something similar. Compassion is the key to enlightenment. It's really not that different from Christianity."

Sam's father looked at me as if I were about to catch fire.

Lucas pulled at my arm. I looked down to see my son's alarmed face. "Mom, what's wrong with Buddha?"

"Nothing, Lucas," I replied. "There's nothing wrong with Buddha."

"Then, why can't we eat at the table?" Lucas rubbed his stomach. "I'm really hungry."

"Of course we can." I turned to Sam's parents. "I will move the statue into the den."

I reached up and hefted Buddha into my arms. As I walked past Sam's parents, I tried to match the statue's beatific expression. But behind my Buddha smile, I was seething—at the bigotry of Sam's parents, at having to subject my son to intolerance, at Sam for looking so miserable.

I was deeply triggered. The superior attitude of Sam's

parents whipped me straight back to Grade 3. To the outcast. Freshly arrived in Canada, I spent recess and lunch by myself, watching my classmates play, wondering why they laughed at me and ran away. Even after I learned the language, I did not understand the unspoken hierarchy of the playground. I wasn't invited to parties and sleepovers until I started playing by their rules. I learned to ditch the fragrant leftovers my mother packed to join the other kids in the cafeteria for bland food. I abandoned my mother tongue and spoke only English. I learned not to mention my family because the other kids didn't care where Taiwan was, even after I explained it wasn't the same as Thailand, that we spoke different languages and had different traditions. They waved aside my explanations. They only wanted to tell me what they knew, what they liked, what they cared about. I let them dominate. I internalized their superiority so they would let me in.

I knew better now. I wasn't a kid anymore, but I was feeling like an outcast again, here, in my own house. I knew I was failing spectacularly with Sam's parents. They could not see past their judgement. I was outside their circle of grace. Instead of a loving home, they saw an unholy one. To them, Buddha was an imposter. My inferiority complex came surging back, only now, my shame verged on white-hot rage.

I kept it in. I would not argue with our guests in front of

Lucas. Besides, it was futile. To a thumper, there was only one supreme being. Theirs was the one true god, all others were counterfeit, irrelevant, dangerous.

Jesus.

My botched attempt at hospitality was followed, predictably, by entreaties from Sam's parents to take us to church. They would love to see me and Lucas again, they said. I made feeble excuses. Lucas had a winter concert. I had a lingering cough. My parents sometimes called on Sundays.

Then came the invitation for Christmas.

"I think they're extending an olive branch," Sam said.

"More like a booby trap." I still smarted from our disastrous dinner.

"But it's Christmas," Sam said. "I know my folks are hard to take, but family is family." For someone who had renounced all religion, I was surprised Sam was so enthusiastic about the holiday. Sam promised we needn't stay long. He gave me a cheesy grin. "Just long enough to introduce the love of my life to the rest of my family."

I considered my own family growing up. Even though my parents didn't celebrate, they let me and my siblings decorate the house with gold and silver tinsel. They even bought us a tabletop tree, painted white to imitate the snow that rarely fell in Vancouver. One year, my mother even tried roasting a turkey. The huge bird was dry. I preferred the fried rice and pork belly with braised greens. After everyone had over-eaten, my father pulled out a deck of cards and taught us blackjack and poker. We gambled with peanut shells. When I started losing, I broke the shells into smaller pieces to stay in the game.

Since my parents and siblings had moved back to Taiwan, Lucas and I had little family around.

"Okay, fine." I made a face at Sam. "But if your dad starts preaching again, I'll scream."

Even before our car came to a complete stop in the parents' driveway, there was no mistaking their house. Christmas lights outlined the roof and every window of the two-storey home. Lawn angels ushered a winding path through the boxwood to the front door. I could hear "The First Noël" coming from the tall maples in the front yard, the notes floating like snowflakes from invisible speakers. Sam rang the doorbell as I nervously smoothed Lucas's hair.

The door opened and Sam's mother greeted us, her smile a wreath of welcome. "Merry Christmas, my dears. I'm so glad you're here." I stood stiffly for a hug and flashed her my best Buddha smile.

Inside, potted poinsettias in red and cream made a forest for three waist-high statues of robed men carrying presents to the crèche. On downy-looking straw, Baby Jesus was asleep, with Joseph, Mary, and a flock of docile-looking animals looking on. I had to admit the manger scene trumped my shoe display.

The house was full of people, their chatter competing with Handel's *Messiah* in the background. The smell of turkey and candied yams filled the air.

Lucas made a beeline for the decorated tree in the living room. A thick blue spruce dominated the room, its boughs trimmed with twinkling lights and tiny angels holding tiny chorus books. At the top, a large white angel presided, her halo grazing the ceiling.

"Woah, Mom, look! Now that's a serious tree." Lucas added our wrapped gifts to the ring of presents and pretended not to read the other tags.

Sam disappeared into the kitchen with my offering for the table: pan-seared Brussels sprouts with parmesan cheese. Sam had laughed when I squeezed lemon juice over the sprouts to hold in their vibrant green. "My family won't recognize your creation. Mom boils them for a week. I used to think eating sprouts was punishment for our sins."

I looked around. The walls of the living room were adorned with framed cross-stitch made by Sam's mother. Her devotion was obvious in each painstaking stitch of coloured thread through starched linen, thousands of repetitions to form the words Love, Joy, Peace and, at the top, Faith. In the middle of the room was an oval coffee table, its centrepiece the Holy Bible. The gold lettering on black leather caught the glow from a real log burning in the fireplace. The mantel was covered in white tulle like a blanket of snow for more angels, their wings spread and ready for ascension. I found myself averting my gaze from the multitude of angels, just as Sam's parents had done when they encountered Buddha in my house.

I took a deep breath and wondered when the ambush would come.

Sam returned from the kitchen and swept me and Lucas over to meet his aunts and uncles, cousins and neighbours. A heady swirl of names and smiling faces. There were twenty or more of us that night. I watched in amazement as Sam's parents served everyone, filled glasses with more punch, handed out presents to Lucas and me.

When it was time to sit down for Christmas dinner, Sam's father presided at the head of the long and laden table. He stood to give the blessing—for God's goodness, for the bounty that He provided, for the many hands that prepared the food and, most of all at Christmas, for the blessing of family. At this, he paused and hunted around the table for Sam and me, fixing us with a stern look.

Under the table, Sam squeezed my hand. I squeezed back.

Earlier in the day, Sam and I had decided to get married in the new year. We laughed that we could at least cross one sin off his parents' list, though Lord only knows how they would react to a civil ceremony. It was Christmas, and we weren't going to upstage one of the holiest days of the year for Sam's parents.

The blessing went on. And on. I tuned out and watched the gravy form a thin skin that would need to be discarded later.

Next to me, I felt Lucas fidget in his chair. One of his legs began to bounce and I clamped a hand on his knee. I glared at him to stop. Lucas crossed his eyes at me, then rolled them round and round. I snorted out loud.

A roomful of eyes looked over at me, appraising, judging, disapproving.

Sam's father cleared his throat and continued.

When we finally got to eat, the meal was delicious. But I could scarcely finish my plate of food. I could feel Sam's parents sizing me up from down the table, figuring out how they would save me and my poor child.

After everyone had had seconds and thirds, the kids disappeared downstairs to watch *How The Grinch Stole Christmas*. I offered to help Sam's aunts clear the table, but Sam's mother waved me aside, "No dear, you are our special guest tonight." I felt a touch at my elbow. Sam's father. He gestured toward the living room and steered me over to an empty loveseat by the fire.

Oh God, here it comes.

I looked around for Sam. He was in an opposite corner, surrounded by his male relatives, in deep conversation.

Sam's father sat down and patted the seat beside him. A log crackled in the fireplace. I eyed the Bible in the middle of the table and lowered myself gingerly to the sofa's edge. Sam's father drew in a quivery breath, as if to gather all his strength and might. Before he could open his mouth, I stuck out my right hand.

"Truce? It's Christmas after all. Let's just agree to disagree."

Sam's father ignored my outstretched hand. His expression was equal parts disdain and pity. "Do you know the meaning of Christmas, young lady?"

I cleared my throat. "What I meant to say was, can we just enjoy the evening? Get into it another time?"

His eyes narrowed. "If by getting into it you mean the very salvation of your soul, then the answer is no. What could be more important than receiving the light of our Lord on Christmas?"

Christ Almighty.

I looked toward Sam, willing him to come over.

Sam's father followed my gaze. "Exactly. Sam." He shook

his head. "And you. What the two of you are doing is wrong. Very wrong. You are hurting not just yourselves, but your son too."

My heart quickened in my temples. "Please leave Lucas out of this."

"Don't you wish the best for your son?"

I ignored his ridiculous question. "Sir, exactly what are Sam and I doing that's so wrong?"

"The way you live, the way you are living . . ." His voice trailed off.

I waited. I wanted him to say it.

He reached for the Bible like a crutch. Without even opening it, he began to quote verse: God's intentions for man, for man and woman, the sin of adultery, the sanctity of marriage and commitment.

I squirmed as the old man preached. I felt like confessing our wedding plans. Maybe that would stop him. Probably not. The Bible didn't exactly sanction second marriages unless one's first spouse had died. I wasn't going to qualify there either.

Sam's father let out another trembling sigh. Suddenly, he looked a lot older.

"Please let me put it another way. I will admit that you would not have been my choice for Sam. But I am not blind. I can see that my son loves you very much and loves

Lucas like his own. But the way you live is . . . is the path to damnation."

I wanted to get up and leave, but something in the old man's demeanour held me there. His expression had changed, his pity and superiority replaced by desperation. Fear perhaps?

He pressed the Bible into my hands.

"Open your heart to God. You will learn that life on earth is nothing compared to the Kingdom of Heaven. The life ever after." His eyes beseeched mine. "Do you understand, my child? I want nothing more than for my family to be together—forever."

Something illuminated inside me.

Sam's father was afraid of losing his son. I thought of Lucas and realized Sam's father only wanted what all parents want, to protect their child from harm. What could be more terrifying than Hell's eternal fire? What was more unbearable than separation from those we love?

I nodded. Yes. I couldn't believe, but I understood.

Back when Lucas's father and I were still pretending to hold our marriage together, even as our periods apart lengthened with each business trip, Lucas sensed the deep rupture in our home. If we fought in front of him, Lucas would get in between us and jump up and down until we stopped. Then he'd grab our fingers and force us into a handshake. "There, now you're friends again." When we could pretend no longer, we told Lucas our love for him would never change, just our living arrangements. We took pains to repeat that none of it was his fault. But blame was not what mattered to Lucas. He cared only that he would never have us together again.

I smiled at Sam's father, still holding onto the Bible I had no intention of opening. I had already read parts of it and found the god within to be angry and unforgiving. I preferred my gentle Buddha.

The fire radiated warmth. It occurred to me that Sam's parents were better than their god. They were caring and kind, like the best Buddhists I knew. Of course, our gods would clash and there would be more sermons and more arguments. But what family didn't fight?

I pictured my perpetually beaming Buddha at home. Perhaps I could be patient too, calmly holding my ground with a serene smile. Compassion didn't have to equal capitulation. It could be a way to hold peace and—dare I hope?—love.

Furby Call Centre

GORAN YERKOVICH

Item #: 0103439482 / Subject Line: Item Never Arrived / Date: 12-24-05 Time: 7:04pm: "To whom it may concern: my item never arrived! I placed the winning bid over two weeks ago. It's now 7pm on Christmas Eve! This is devastating! I want my item! I want my FURBY!"

I was an 'on-probation-waiting-for-full-hire-status-and-benefits' Customer Service Representative (CSR1) for Team Canada at a call centre. Probation could last three to six months if your metrics were low. Technically, I wasn't even an employee yet. I was contracting for a recruitment firm, without full salary or benefits. The pay was $12 per hour. So I was poor. I was worried I might get fired. But I wasn't alone. The call centre had around four hundred down-and-out employees working on four floors.

The reps did two types of jobs. CSR2s reviewed live seller listings and took down bad sellers. CSR1s, junior staff like me, answered emails regarding buyer and seller complaints. They worked late. They worked holidays. They worked Christmas Eve.

I didn't know it at the time, but back in 2003, Furbies

*

experienced a massive resurgence in popularity. They were small interactive furry pet dolls that could sing, talk, and respond to touch. But their ultimate feature—to develop language skills and react to humans—gave them something special: apparent intelligence.

Furbies communicated with one another without eye contact, via an infrared port located between their eyes. We communicated via low whispers, Microsoft Outlook, Windows 2000, and state-of-the-art productivity metrics. Furbies were designed to engage with their owners and the environment at all times. And as we moved deeper into the holiday season, we were responding to thirty to sixty emails per hour, twenty-four hours per day, for every shift. So while Furbies were allowed to play games, dance, and express emotions, we were asked to keep our seats and answer the endless barrage of email complaints with generic responses from Microsoft Excel macros, designed to make our correspondence appear human. Not that there were that many humans around this particular night.

Seven rows of workstations away, I could see our supervisor step in and out of his glass-walled office to collect papers from the large printer. He was right next to the only sensor-active entrance door on our floor. This meant, along with the software, he could easily track our every move.

It was early in the shift, but I needed to use the washroom. I paused from my emails, changed my status to 'Break_Washroom,' grinned as I passed him, and swiped my ID Card. I couldn't tell what had been printed, but some pages were on official company letterhead. Those must have been job offers: full status, benefits, and a raise. The other sheets were pink.

Under dimmed lights, I stared into the bathroom mirror. My spiked brown hair remained gelled in place, but my new bright blue collared dress shirt was slightly wrinkled. I tried to press the wrinkles out with a damp hand with minimal success. I used too much water. It soaked down into my new black pants near the groin area, which then required seven or eight paper towels that smudged shaker-sized white flecks across both top and crotch.

Rick had his office door closed when I tiptoed back to my desk. I changed my status back to "Active_Email_ Queue_Buyers_Canada" and then stood again and stepped to my left. At the end of our aisle, a communal basket was filled with silver-wrapped candy and chocolates. They sparkled under our fluorescent department lights. I grabbed a handful and dropped them on my desk next to my half-eaten dinner and began to methodically unwrap a piece of white chocolate wrapped in festive emerald green tin foil.

"Hey, what's wrong with you? You want to get fired?"

Vince, only an arm's length away, slouched in his chair

to my right. He had recently arrived from Hong Kong and told me once he'd been cut off by his father and needed this job, for now. His black turtleneck matched his thick black-framed glasses which, from my angle, hid his eyes. He remained focused on his screen while his shoulders strained and his fingers continued to type.

"It's Christmas Eve. We can relax." I popped another chocolate and sat back in my chair.

It didn't matter that my current email stats blinked in red to display '20/Hr' —ten less than the expected minimum hourly response average—a number I'd struggled to maintain for almost three months since I arrived.

"You sure? You know who our supervisor is tonight? What he did last Christmas?"

"That's a rumour. I don't think he actually fired anyone on Christmas Eve."

I ignored the pop-ups and live email on my screen and looked around. Gold and silver tinsel was wrapped around my workstation. It glittered and waved from the heat vents pushing much needed warm air into the office. The main floor of our washed-out beige and diamond patterned carpet matched the mottled grey office partitions. The space was long and rectangular with over fifty nearly identical workstations: chairs, desktop computers, keyboards, and file trays. Each workstation also had short raised glass dividers no more than ten inches in height, designed to create the illusion of a dedicated miniature office space, which some agents happily nested into, displaying their multicoloured lights, banners, and a wide array of random dolls, badges, nerf guns, and other toys.

The day before, the floor was filled with the hustle and buzz of Team Canada agents but tonight most seats sat empty and quiet. On some desks I did see new oversized steel-plated name tags. I looked at a few. They belonged to people I interacted with in the coffee station or cafeteria. For the most part, they had limited social skills, some unable to hold a conversation. But the new name tags declared that some were in fact a class above the rest—those fortunate enough, talented enough, disciplined enough, to reach permanent employment status.

"I'm telling you, Rick fired someone over Christmas Eve last year. What do you think he was printing over there? Awards?" Vince continued with his emails and spoke in a low whisper.

I emptied the red and green Lindt chocolate wrappers from my slightly wet pant pockets and placed the wrappers into the plastic garbage bin only a few inches from my keyboard. "He was printing on letterhead too."

"Great. So, what are your email stats now for the month?"

"Thirty-one," I said, finally prepared to look at my next email.

∗

"I'm at sixty-five, aiming for seventy. Does your thirty-one include tonight's totals? Month averages never include the current day."

I stared at my current stats and did some mental calculations. Vince was right.

I opened a different tab on my screen and looked at my stats again. If my numbers did not improve tonight, my monthly average would be around twenty-eight or twenty-nine. I'd be eligible for dismissal. "Damn. I might be in trouble."

Vince said, "Try to pull emails in the queue that look the same. It's faster. The same thing over and over. And stop personalizing it."

"Yeah, I will. But I like to personalize mine. Way better that way. Our customers don't want to interact with robots."

Vince made a sound that seemed Furbish to me, like a sneeze or noise I could not yet understand.

"Well, be careful. I heard Rick's trying to get promoted."

"Aren't we all?" I began to type a hello message and something about Furbies into the body of an email to one of our customers.

"I mean, he doesn't want problems. There's a vacant Senior Manager position. I think the last guy was fired because his overall team had bad stats. Or something like that."

"Great. No one is safe here."

Item # 0100337442 / Subject line: Item Issue – Refund / Date: 12-24-05 Time: 7:40pm: "Hi, I received my Furby a month ago and it worked fine but now I think it's haunted or really hungry. It wakes up at night, makes strange sounds, and then asks for food. How do I get a refund?

Another Furby email. Before I could respond my cell phone buzzed on quiet mode. I flipped my Nokia open. It was Mom. I hunched to make myself as small as possible.

"Merry Christmas, Gorane!" She used the affectionate, diminutive version of my name. "Oh my God, how are you, my son? My poor son. Are you still working now? On Christmas Eve?"

"Merry Christmas, Mom! Yes, I'm at work. I told you I took the shift. It's double pay and..."

"Oh my God, Gorane, I told you not to move to Vancouver. You should have just stayed in Calgary with us. All your friends have jobs in oil and gas now, and they're married, and you don't even have ..."

"Mom. I'm good. I can't talk long. I'm at work."

"Okay, okay. We are all sitting here in the dining room and thinking of you. Your sister is here with her family, the neighbours are over, and, you know, the usual friends. We have so much food left over. I'm so sorry you're not with us tonight."

I pictured Christmas Eve dinner from a few years ago, the last time I was home: Mom and Dad's dark-oak Queen

Anne covered in one of Mom's red Walmart tablecloths that should have been thrown away decades ago. Seated around it, family and good friends.

"It's okay Mom, don't worry. So what did you make for dinner?"

"Oh, Gorane, everything as usual. My spareribs, cabbage rolls, ham, roast potatoes, the turkey, and Donna brought her bacon broccoli pasta salad that you love, and Anita brought a Skor bar cake again. Do you remember this cake? She said you loved it, but I can't remember. I don't think it's very good."

"Yes Mom, Anita makes that cake a lot. I think it's Donna's recipe. But Mom, your cakes are still the best." I could hear my sister shout about cake in the background.

"I know. Thank you, Gorane. And as usual, your father is still arguing with Renato again about the best way to make homemade wine. Or olive oil. Or something about building cabinets. Or what the best deer meat is, and how to make it. It's always something. They're so crazy, those guys."

I laughed. Dad and Renato. They both knew the answers to everything. Each Christmas they bickered non-stop but they'd always invite each other over, year after year.

"Gorane, what about you? What are you eating there tonight? I hope you're eating okay. Did the company you work for make you something?"

"Don't worry Mom. Yes . . . they made us a nice turkey dinner here, with all the trimmings." Still crouched to the side, I looked over at Vince who paused on his keyboard and turned his neck down toward my sad and half-eaten micro-waved Hungry-Man-Meat-Loaf-Gravy dinner. He turned back to his screen without eye contact and gave a sour smile.

"Ah, that's nice, Gorane. I'm glad you at least got some turkey for Christmas, but hopefully it's good. Did they give you lots of gravy? I know how much you like your gravy."

"Yes, Mom, they gave us gravy. I'm good. I told you not to worry. Okay. I have to go. You guys enjoy your meal, and I will call you tomorrow. I'll be here late, until midnight, so I'll call whenever I wake up tomorrow. Don't worry, okay?"

"Was it the powdered gravy? I hope it wasn't powdered."

"Mom, I have to go. Love you." I looked back up at my screen and the Buyer email queue. More emails were in. My stats were even lower. 19/Hr. The number was in red.

"Okay, my son. You know I love you very much. Your sister is here. She's wishing you a Merry Christmas too. She's asking if you used the money she sent to buy a proper bed finally?"

My sister had sent me $400 when they found out I'd been sleeping on an air mattress for the last six months. "Yes Mom, tell Anita I bought a bed a few weeks ago. Tell her I said thanks again for the money. I'll call her tomorrow."

Just then, I noticed a shadow. Someone next to me, to my left. Vince straightened in his seat while he continued to type. I corrected my position in the chair and ended the call.

"Hey Goran, the Buyer emails have piled up. That's your queue. Need to get back at it." It was Rick, our supervisor. He had that strange smile on his face.

I could see Rick with a folder in his hand and a pink paper inside.

"Goran get the queue numbers back up and then come by my office at 9 pm sharp, please. You have little over an hour."

Rick looked down at the mess on my desk. The half-eaten food. A plastic fork with a tiny piece of meatloaf still on it, and down farther on the floor, Lindt wrappers that had missed their target.

An intense balled-up glow of silver and gold reflected from Rick's glossy and spotless black dress shoes. His laces were double-knotted.

> *Item # 0100337442 / Subject line: Item Issue – Refund / Date: 12-24-05 Time: 8:20pm: Hi, I need a refund. There's some sort of battery drain issue with my Furby. Even after I put in fresh batteries, my Furby rapidly drains power. Like it's half dead. Or in some sort of arrested development.*

I had increased my email output thanks to Vince. I

searched for keywords that linked to pre-written responses and merged them together into the emails with only a minimum amount of personalization. To my surprise, the work was now mindless and I daydreamed back to how this started. How I ended up at work on Christmas Eve in a place like this.

After two years abroad, I returned to Canada, but instead of going to Calgary where I'd lived most of my life, my destination was Vancouver. I had told myself it was a place of fern-covered forest floors, mountain tops, kelp, orcas, and whales, green grass all year round, and Peking Duck. But the truth was, when I first left home, I promised myself and my parents that I would be a great success. It didn't go that way, so I couldn't show my face. Not until I had something to celebrate.

After two months of crashing at a friend's place, sleeping on an air mattress on his dining room floor, I moved into a basement suite with two new roommates I barely knew. Steve had a photographic memory and was a massive Liverpool Football Club supporter with tattoos that covered his arms, legs, and back. He preferred to be called Ste and explained that he had been part of a boyband in the UK with one radio hit called "Cream," which he said reached the Top-40 charts in Poland.

Ste also had a digestion problem, or at least he did on the

flight over from London to Vancouver, where, by chance, I met him and his best friend, Baby-David. Dave received the 'Baby' in this name from his sisters because of his boyish appearance and ability to never get in trouble, even when it was his fault. Baby-David was an all-around nice guy who could have been a chef, but had planned to find a job in IT once he settled in Vancouver.

When I called them a few months after my return to Canada, neither Ste nor Dave seemed to mind that I had a small pile of debt, no money, no job connections, and little relevant work experience: they were happy to take me in.

At about the same time that I moved into the empty basement with Ste and Baby-David, I landed the job as a Customer Service Representative. But I was still poor, only just making monthly rent. I didn't have any paid vacation, and couldn't afford to fly to Calgary even if I wanted to.

> *Item # 0100337442 / Subject line: Item Issue –*
> *Refund / Date: 12-24-05 Time: 8:40pm: Hi, I need*
> *a refund. I bought a Furby for my kids. But now it's*
> *exhibiting some erratic behaviour, like strange move-*
> *ments, and inconsistent reactions. Like it laughs*
> *when it shouldn't. How do I get my refund? Thanks*
> *for your time. And Merry Christmas!*

As the hour almost passed, I had fully replaced my overly

personalized approach. No part of my emails were now personalized. To my amazement, I slogged through them in rapid succession.

While my macro copy-and-paste activity continued, another Furby fact popped into my head: Furbies communicated in something called Furbish, which would seem like gibberish to anyone else. But we were supplied manuals provided by their creators and they implied the toy's communication approach somehow gave customers exactly what they needed, even if nonsense. It seemed that Furbish, if applied correctly, made perfect sense for this job too.

I thought back to my last encounter with Rick almost a month ago.

"Goran, we need to talk. You've been late twice in November already. This is bad. I know you just requested to take the Christmas shifts, but you might not even make it that far. Overall, honestly, this is not good. There are some poor scores here. Poor. Poor. Poor. If you're late again, we can let you go. You know that, right?" Rick's thin-framed glasses slid down from his flattened nose while he awaited my reply. He wore that strange smile.

"I'm sorry, I caught the Skytrain and the bus this morning. My bus was late. Usually they get me here just before 8:00am."

"If you start your shift at 8:00am, you should aim to arrive at 7:45 or 7:50 at the latest."

"I don't have much of a choice. I don't have a car. And the earlier bus would get me here at 7:20 or 7:30. And I was told I couldn't start early. Just at 8:00."

"You know the rules. We talk about this at team huddles all the time. Three late arrivals and we decide if it's a write-up or a straight dismissal. And to be honest, like I said, your metrics aren't so good, either. They've actually gotten worse. And now two lates."

"I was only late by one minute this morning. And I personalize my responses to make them better."

"See this timecard stamp?"

"Yeah. 8:06am. I was one minute late. Do you really count that?"

"It's six minutes late."

"But you said we have five minutes' grace period. If we start at 8:00am, we can start at 8:05?"

"Yes, true, we give everyone that buffer. But if you're late, the buffer is excluded. Goran, your ranking is one of the lowest of the new hires. You struggle with First Response Resolution and Number of Responses per Hour. Really low. Unfortunately, we might be forced to let some people go by the end of the month, if they don't make it past probation. I know it's Christmas soon, but this is an important time of year. And we have a new class coming in soon. Fresh blood."

"I'm sorry. I'll work on my metrics. And I won't be late again."

> *Item # 0100944449 / Subject line: Item Issue – Refund / Date: 12-24-05 Time: 8:59pm: Hi, I bought a Green Furby Baby and it had a cute high-pitched voice but now the voice has stopped. How can I take care of a baby Furby if I can never hear it cry? Can I ask for Refund?*

The clock struck 9:00pm. With "Dance of the Sugar Plum Fairy" in the background, I answered what might have been my very last Furby email. I swivelled in my chair to look at the coworkers behind me and to my right, who typed, sneezed, and coughed their way through more emails.

It had dawned on me that this place was the land of Misfit Toys: engineers, cinematographers, scientists, former math prodigies, and other helpless people with communication, business, or fine arts degrees had all been marooned here on this email productivity iceberg with no way off and no way home.

There was Anne, a former scientist who had run out of funds from the Federal government and who could no longer do her x-ray experiments at the local university. There was Tony, Cevat, and Richard, all engineers with honours degrees who couldn't find relevant work. There were even two cinematographers both hoping to get funded for new films they planned to write, shoot, and produce.

They said, like the rest of us here, this was just a temporary thing. We'd all be off to something better soon. And yet, I discovered four or five years had passed for some. It seemed, for many, this might have been the end of their road.

I scanned all those seated beside me. I didn't see any security staff. If I was about to get fired, one of these staff members might have already been assigned to come to my desk with a box they would pack while I spoke with Rick. Then the box would be given to me at the front door on my way out. That's how it was always done. If it happened, it'd be the last time I'd see this desk, this office, and possibly everyone inside it.

I placed my status on 'Meeting_Other' and grabbed my cell phone and jacket. "Well. Thanks for all your help, Vince. If this is it, see you around."

"Yup." Vince turned his head slightly to give a nod and then continued with his emails.

Had I ever seen Vince's eyes? I wasn't sure. "Well, you can have my tinsel."

"Right."

"Seriously though, can you make sure they don't throw my stuff away? They should put it in a box and bring it to me."

"Yeah. I know. I'll watch."

"So, you think I'm getting fired . . . right?"

"Probably. Maybe."

"Great."

"Maybe if you're lucky, you're stuck here until midnight with the rest of us."

"Win–win." I stood and took one last mental picture of my desk, the empty rows, the half-lit lights and decorations, and our small group huddled together. I pocketed a few more chocolates and walked towards my 9:00pm.

Rick's door was wide open. There were no Christmas decorations, no picture frames of family, no artwork on the wall. Only two chairs, a floor lamp, and a large yellow desk with manila folders spread across. Rick sat, pen in hand, with one folder open.

"Hey, come in. Close the door behind you. Why'd you bring your jacket?"

"Oh, I might go outside after. For a short break." I sat down in the chair across from him.

"Okay . . . But it's freezing rain right now. It might be a white Christmas after all. But anyway, thanks for the hustle over the last hour. Queue numbers are better.

"But listen we need to talk and I'll keep this quick. You

know your email stats haven't been great. They hover right near the bottom of our benchmarks."

I nodded and noticed the folder in front of Rick had my name on it.

Rick flipped to one page in my monthly benchmark score results. "These are your latest numbers . . ." He paused to show me. "Okay, I'll cut to the chase. We're not firing you. But your numbers are still borderline, so we're not hiring you either. Not until we see some steady improvement. The good news is I was able to pull some strings, and we'll be able to grant you another three-month probationary period. That means you keep your job through the recruitment company, but your pay stays the same, and no benefits yet. But you'll have one more opportunity to get things in line."

"Yeah. Okay. Thanks."

"I know this isn't the news you are looking for, but I didn't want you worrying over Christmas. Just keep those numbers way above thirty. Get them to forty, fifty. Keep working with Vince. Okay?"

"Okay. Thank you. I'll get my numbers up."

"I know this isn't your dream job. But it's your job. Just do better next year."

"Sounds good."

"Okay, good. So, I don't know if you noticed, but there's

cake in the kitchen. I brought it in. Could you help me hand it out tonight? We'll bring it to everyone's desks. Celebrate a bit together. It is Christmas, after all."

"Thanks. But I got a bunch of Furby emails. It was strange. Are Furbies back or something?"

"I have no idea."

With Rick's permission we all placed our statuses on 'Break_Other,' and for a glorious twenty minutes we cut cake, shared stories, and ate together, the ten of us, our little crew of misfit toys, who all worked Christmas Eve that night. Anne shared the story of how a few months back security was called in when she wore tiger-balm to the office and maintenance was convinced there was a serious natural gas leak right above her desk.

I finished my shift and scrambled across puddles of fresh ice as snowflakes fell. Past 1:00am, back at my basement apartment, Ste and Baby-David sat on our secondhand couches as they watched *National Lampoon's Christmas Vacation*. Both had their feet up on our living room coffee table: a basement closet door we'd removed from a bedroom that we'd placed over two large cardboard boxes covered with one of Mom's Walmart tablecloths.

Ste welcomed me back with a drink, while Baby-David explained he had decided to make a turkey. He had wrapped the leftovers in tin foil and placed it in the oven. And to my astonishment there was homemade gravy in a pot on the stove.

In my room, with the radio left on, an old choir rendition of "Silent Night" played as I dropped my bag off and stared at my partially inflated air mattress with clean bed sheets and my pillow neatly folded on top.

I hadn't been able to tell Mom I'd spent the money from my sister to pay bills and buy some new clothes for work instead—like the clothes I had worn that night.

I wasn't sure how long I'd last at this job, or what I'd do next, but I was determined to dress the part, and to at least take the job more seriously until I figured it out. And I promised myself I would never work another Christmas Eve again.

I walked back to the kitchen, took my turkey meal with extra gravy, grabbed my ice-cold drink, and moved to the floor in the living room next to Ste and Baby-David. No one spoke for the rest of the night, in either English or Furbish. We didn't need to. We understood each other just fine.

Shelter

JENNIFER ALLEN

The bunk beds did make the first night a little better.

Mom spoke in the bedroom doorway with a worker who hadn't smiled once since we arrived. She reminded me of my grandmother but grumpier. And if I knew one thing about grumpy grandmas, it was to stay out of their hair.

I inched away from them and closer to the bunk beds. I wanted to stake my claim before Stephanie, my six-year-old sister, could. She already had a loft playhouse bed back at home and was used to sleeping in something fun. I slept on an antique hospital bed. Its metal frame creaked and rattled every time I rolled over. I was always afraid I would cut myself on the sharp edges.

So sure, the bunk was secondhand and covered in another kid's marker but it beat what I had. Also I was the oldest by three years. I remember deciding I definitely deserved the top bunk over Stephanie.

I would throw my Cabbage Patch Kid on the top bunk before Stephanie could even open her mouth. I just needed the shelter worker to leave so I could call it.

I sidled to the window and pulled back the curtain. We

were on the second floor of an old house halfway up a hill. I could see the city below, a traffic light at the bottom of the hill, and an orange bridge off in the distance. Colourful lights and snowman decorations lit up the houses nearby, creating a warm seasonal glow. The storefronts, restaurants, and the lead-zinc smelter across the city flashed and blurred into a mix of reds, whites, and industrial oranges.

In the distance, tiny pinpricks lit up a handful of houses. These were my favourite. They reminded me of the quiet times we had at home in the winter.

Our tree this particular year was the best. Mom drove my sister and me to a wide-open forest early that December. She grabbed my father's axe from the back of the pickup and swung at its trunk from every direction. Finally the thing fell down along with an empty bird's nest hidden in the branches. Mom cradled the nest and said we had our first decoration.

At home, Mom had taught us how to make a construction-paper chain garland that we'd draped around the tree. She took us to ceramics classes to paint our own decorations. I painted animals like birds, mice, and a family of cats. Stephanie and I also brought home things we'd made from school. From start to finish, this tree belonged to my sister and me, and it made us proud.

The worker explained the house rules to my mother

while my sister kept her eye on me. Mom was responsible for our breakfasts and lunches. Food was in the fridge and the pantry. A chef would take care of dinner. She usually made meals like vegetable soup, spaghetti, and meatloaf. The shelter had one television but no cable TV because they didn't want anyone fighting over the channels. Finally, no men allowed—not even her father.

Us kids weren't allowed to run up and down the stairs. We also had to stay out of the other bedrooms even if they were empty. And most importantly: never ever give out the shelter's address or phone number. Stephanie and I were good kids. Everyone always told our parents how well-behaved and quiet we were. This woman was different, and I didn't like how she was already upset at us for no reason. I suddenly had the urge to run up and down all the stairs around and check out every single room. I wanted to see if they had bunk beds, too. I think not knowing why she directed her anger at us kids crushed me because we depended on a warmth and comfort we never saw. I just wanted to give her a real reason to be mad. But I knew better.

The worker said the shelter had a playroom in the basement. It had all kinds of toys donated from kids who no longer needed them. The last time I'd dug through a basement full of toys was at my cousin's. She'd grown too old for her Strawberry Shortcake dolls and let my sister and me each pick a doll, one at a time. Many had no clothes, had messy hair, and had lost their scent altogether. Some even had black spots—what Mom later called mould—growing on their legs.

I didn't want other people's broken toys. I wanted all the toys I had back at home. The My Little Pony Paradise Estate still had all its pieces, my Barbies had their original dresses, and my own Strawberry Shortcake dolls smelled like they were supposed to. I figured it was like this: if a kid didn't want to play with their old, broken toys, then why would I? Why did charity have to be so dirty?

The basement also had a donation room full of used clothing, said the worker. Mom said she'd find us kids new outfits in the morning. But I wasn't about to wear someone else's clothes for the same reason I wasn't about to play with someone else's toys. Too filthy and uncared for. The outfits I brought from home were just fine. But in the end, none of this mattered because I knew we'd be out of there soon. My family always celebrated the holidays together.

Before she left, the worker said one last thing: the shelter would separate us into different rooms after a week. They wanted to free up the only family-sized bedroom in the house for future families. My sister and I would stay at one end of the hall and my mother at the other.

No. We couldn't be away from her. Why would they

separate us kids from our mom? I'd once gotten lost in a department store and sobbed for fifteen minutes straight. Sure, we were still under the same roof but that didn't stop me from panicking when I couldn't find her. Finally a kind woman brought me to customer support where they paged my mom, who showed up half-relieved, half-angry. The thought of not seeing my mom across the room from me in a strange women's shelter scared me. The worker closed the old wooden door behind her with a click, which made me jump.

I tossed my doll on the top bunk and called it. Stephanie was in no mood to fight. Instead, she waited by the bottom bunk for our mother to tuck her in for the second time that night.

I climbed up top and studied the view: pale green walls, a wooden dresser, and my mother's single bed. Being up high wasn't as great as I thought it would be. I pulled the covers over me and laid my head on the pillow. The sheets smelled nothing like the ones at home. They were a different kind of clean, so that even in the dark I couldn't pretend I was in my own bed.

I thought of my father coming home to an empty trailer that night and missed him so much. I couldn't fully understand why we'd left—especially tonight. As far as I knew, my dad was just like the other dads in the village: he drove a pickup truck, he visited the bar, and listened to loud rock music with the windows down. In fact, he was better because he could weld, which meant he could make anything. He also built his own cars for the demolition derby and won first place every year. And sometimes he'd take Stephanie and me four-wheeling in his truck through the mountains.

In the summer, however, Mom said he'd been hurting her in private. It had been going on for a while. She even had to see a doctor. This didn't make any sense to me because he was always around and I never saw him do or say anything wrong. My mother swore me to secrecy that we'd leave someday but wouldn't tell me where or when. We never spoke of it again. In fact, I had forgotten all about her plan by September. If anyone at school asked about my family, I would have told them we were happy because I thought we were.

I tucked myself deeper into the top bunk as my sister below me snored. Holidays always brought families together. Mine would be no different. I couldn't wait to leave the shelter.

Toys covered every surface in the playroom: shelves, tables, window sills, and all over the orange, shag carpet. Board games had been abandoned halfway through, LEGO had been taken apart and left in pieces, and stuffed animals looked like they'd been dropped and forgotten.

"What a mess," said Mom.

She was right. We kicked our way through a mountain of toys just to get to the couch. Stephanie dug through a pile of dolls at our feet. She pulled up a few sad-looking ones then tossed them aside. I, too, had no interest in dolls with homemade haircuts, new faces drawn on them, and missing body parts.

Next to her, however, was an action figure with long red hair and blue eyeshadow. I bent down and picked her up. She was She-Ra's friend and one of the original Princesses of Power. I didn't have Castaspella in my collection yet.

She still had her yellow skirt, but was missing my favourite part: the sparkly, spinning disc she wore on her back. It temporarily hypnotized enemies, which was by far one of the most interesting weapons the princesses had.

I wanted to take her home where she would live at the Crystal Castle with the others. No one would miss her. Not in this mess. But as I searched for the disc, I thought about the first and only time I stole: I took a plastic, green-jewelled ring from a drugstore because I wanted to know what it felt like to steal.

Once we left the store, I was so overcome with guilt I threw the ring onto the sidewalk. My babysitter picked it up and gave it to my parents that afternoon when I apologized and confessed to everything. My dad hung the ring on the turn signal of his pickup truck to remind me of what I'd done. I couldn't bring this toy from the shelter back to my father and look him in the eye. I put the action figure down. She was no good without her powers anyway.

On the other side of the playroom, beyond another mountain of toys, was the donation room that doubled as a laundry room. The open concrete space smelled old, cold, and wet. Mom sorted through a cardboard box full of clothing while Stephanie watched. I was more interested in the bathtub-sized sink next to the washer and dryer. I turned on both taps and held my hand underneath but no water came out. The window above it was frozen shut so I tried the wooden door that led outside. I wanted to feel the snow. I wanted fresh air. But the door wouldn't budge no matter how hard I tried.

"Nothing works in this place," I said.

Mom ignored me and told me to pick out some clothes. She already had a growing pile of pants, shirts, and sweaters for my sister and herself. I picked up a winter jacket that smelled like someone else's house and put it back.

"I have clothes at home," I told her.

"You have clothes in your suitcase."

I was the oldest kid, who wasn't used to wearing hand-me-downs and secondhand items. Mom always bought my clothes brand new or sewed them herself. Secondhand stores were for playhouse beds, Nancy Drew novels, and Archie comics. After I refused to pick out anything, Mom said fine and that she'd do it herself.

That's when we met the second worker. A woman with short hair and dangly earrings stood in the doorway holding a laundry basket full of towels. I didn't know how long she'd been there but I did wonder if she heard me say all those bad things about the shelter because she did not look happy.

The woman eyed our mountain of clothing and I knew this was a bad idea because we didn't need any of this stuff. Then she stared at my mother long enough to make me shift in my socks. "Try leaving some for the others," the worker eventually said, before drifting past us.

My mother shot the woman an icy stare but she was too busy at the washing machine to notice. When the woman didn't look back my mother grabbed the massive pile of clothes and said, "Come on, girls," then led us out of the room with her nose in the air. I followed behind with my head hung low.

Mom made us try on the donated clothing in our room. I stood in front of the mirror in a white sweatshirt with a faded rainbow that ran up one arm, across my chest, and down the other arm.

"That looks nice on you," Mom said.

"It has a stain on it," I said.

"Where?"

I showed her what looked like pink nail polish on the cuff.

She rolled the band over. "There. No one will ever know."

I said I would. She told me to stop being so miserable. But I didn't know how.

Mom said she'd try on her donated clothes later because she was going out. She threw on a sheer, black top covered in sequins she had stitched on herself. She usually wore this when going out for dinner with her girlfriends or my father.

"Where are you going?" I asked.

"Out."

"With Dad?" Mom didn't answer.

"When will you be back?"

"Later."

"Will you bring us back something?" Stephanie asked. Mom said yes. I didn't want anything from the store.

In the kitchen, Mom made us peanut butter and strawberry jam sandwiches and set them on the table before kissing us goodbye. After she left, Stephanie and I ran up to our room to watch her through the window. We couldn't find her.

"Bathroom," I said.

We ran to the top floor, climbed onto the toilet seat and looked out the window. We stood on our tiptoes to get a full view of the street. Our mother teetered up the sidewalk in her high heels through ankle-deep snow. After slipping a few times and laughing at herself, she finally made it to a shiny gold car that had been waiting for her. Mom opened the passenger-side door and went to get in but stopped. She said something to the driver, then looked down at her shoes. Mom kicked the snow off her high heels and climbed inside.

The car turned around and drove past the house. I tried to see the driver but only caught a glimpse of a single hairy arm. We watched them, our tiptoes aching, until they were out of sight. I didn't know who this mystery man was or what he wanted with my mother and why. I just knew I hated him.

Stephanie and I returned to the kitchen table and ate our lunch. The worker with the dangly earrings showed up. She sat across from us with a cup of tea in her hands and stared at me the way she had stared at my mother. I edged my chair back a little and took a bite of my sandwich.

"That's a nice shirt," said the woman.

I thanked her.

"Did you get it from the donation room?"

I didn't know what to say because the more I thought about her question, the more I felt trapped. If I said yes, then she'd get mad at me for taking it. If I said no, then she'd get mad at me for lying. So I told her I didn't know.

That night, after Mom finally came back, I let her know about the worker in the kitchen. I told her I was done with the shelter and that I wanted to go home. Christmas was only three days away.

Mom pointed her finger at me and said, "The next time she asks you that question, you tell her 'no.'" She ignored my comment about going home.

"Who was that man you were with?" I asked.

"What man?"

"The one with the gold car."

Mom asked how we knew and I told her we saw them from the bathroom window. My mother said he was just a friend and that his name was Rob. I told her I didn't like him. She said I didn't have to. At least not yet. I had no idea what that meant but I didn't like how it sounded.

Mom went out with Rob again the following night. He took her to dinner at an all-you-can-eat spaghetti restaurant, then to a nightclub called Rosario's.

A third worker let us watch a movie at the shelter. Movie night was a big deal for me because I couldn't remember the last time I'd watched TV. Compared to the others, this worker was younger, prettier, and smiled more. She was my favourite. I thought maybe she was in high school because she reminded me of the babysitters we had back at home.

The worker let us pick any VHS from the Disney collection and said she'd watch it with us. Stephanie and I chose *Lady and the Tramp* because it was the only one we hadn't seen. Then she taught us how to make Jiffy Pop on the stove. My sister and I took turns swirling the frying pan until its top layer inflated into a silver balloon the size of our heads.

The smell of popcorn always made my stomach turn but the popping thrilled me because it usually meant a good time would follow. And because we were the only ones at the shelter that night, we didn't have to share our snack with anyone.

Stephanie and I filled our bowls and took them into the living room where we sat on the couch beside the Christmas tree. I admired the wrapped presents underneath and wondered if any of them were for us. The girl sat across from us in the recliner with her feet kicked up and played the movie.

Halfway into the show, the doorbell rang in the kitchen. The worker looked at me, her eyes wide, and I couldn't tell if she was surprised or afraid or both, which made me nervous. She paused the movie and told us to wait there while she answered the door.

Moments later, a man carrying a camera followed her into the living room. His eyes lit up when he saw us. He said he worked for the newspaper and was writing a story about the Christmas donations. The man held out his camera and asked if we wanted our picture taken. I didn't, but I also didn't think I could say no to him. I thought I'd make him mad after he'd been so happy to see us. I looked at the young worker for help. But she only stood against the wall and watched.

Stephanie followed me to the tree where we both sat cross-legged. The man reached underneath the tree and grabbed two presents, then placed them in our hands. My sister and I looked at each other and our eyes grew big. When the photographer told us to smile, we gave him our biggest, happiest smiles and then he snapped the picture.

I was ready to tear open my gift when the man snatched it from my hands. "These aren't for you," he said, reaching for my sister's. He shoved them back under the tree. The worker let him out. I spent the rest of the movie wondering what I'd done wrong and why the shelter worker didn't help us when the man took the gifts back. Who were they for if not us? It didn't make sense to have a tree with presents underneath and no one to give them to.

The next morning was December 24, and when Mom asked how movie night went, I told her about the photographer and how I was more upset that he'd taken my gift than my picture.

Mom looked at me, her eyes dark like a crow's. "You had your picture taken? For the newspaper?" I said yes.

My mother told my sister and me to stay in the room

while she went downstairs. I covered my ears, too afraid to listen to her argue with one of the workers over something I'd said. All Stephanie and I could do was stare at each other.

Mom came back upstairs, grabbed a suitcase, and threw our clothes in it.

"Where are we going?" I asked.

"The shelter's closed for Christmas. We're going to Grandma and Grandpa's."

I helped her pack. I loved my grandparents. They loved us in return with their too-tight hugs, home-cooked meals, and questions about school. Sometimes Grandma painted my nails or let me paint hers, but most of all she said, "Children should be seen and not heard." That was my cue to watch cable TV, which was something I couldn't wait to do. I'd been missing the holiday specials.

I didn't want to go back to the shelter. I don't think anyone did. But we knew my grandparents' place was too small and crowded. Eventually we'd need a real plan. Until then, we just wanted to enjoy the season.

Grandma had dinner simmering on the stove when we arrived. The mobile home smelled of meat, potatoes, vegetables, and homemade dumplings. I loved her beef stew even though I hated the turnips. Usually she made me eat them, but that night I didn't have to finish my turnips at all.

I wondered what dinner would have been like at the shelter that night. I bet it wasn't as good as this.

The shelter, I thought, was too big. My grandparents' cozy double-wide trailer was warm and all I needed. We weren't separated by old stairs, creaky floors, and cranky women. We were separated by a long hallway with a shag rug where we could yell from the kitchen and the person at the other end of the hall would hear you loud and clear.

My grandparents' home was a home of convenience. Stephanie and I could help ourselves to the refrigerator, the television, and the After Eight chocolates on the table usually reserved for adults.

To its credit, the shelter was in a better part of town. It had shops, parks, and grand two-storey houses nearby. But the junkyard behind my grandparents' trailer park had become a familiar place to my sister and me who were used to playing in rusty barrels, old tires, and abandoned demolition derby cars. I didn't like old, donated clothing and other people's broken toys but I liked getting dirty outside with my sister. The junkyard reminded me of car parts and tools my dad had scattered all over our property.

After we finished our apple crisp, Grandma shooed Grandpa away so we could wrap his gifts. Mom left the room to phone Dad and I couldn't wait to hear all about him. I wanted to know how he was doing and if he missed me as much as I missed him, and if he knew where to find us. I wanted him to come over with our presents and stay the night.

My grandmother set a roll of wrapping paper covered with rosy-cheeked Santa faces and a clear bag of bows on the coffee table. She pulled out Grandpa's gifts she had hidden in the broom closet: plaid shirts, a watch, soap on a rope, and a bottle of Old Spice aftershave. I grabbed the aftershave off the table. I had seen something similar in the bathroom. This was Grandpa's scent and I wanted to wrap it.

But Grandma said wrapping was her job, along with cutting the paper and filling out the labels. She put my sister and me in charge of the tape and bows. I tore off a piece of tape while she measured and cut the paper for the Old Spice, then handed it to her. Once she was done, she handed the wrapped gift back to me.

I dumped the bag of bows on the carpet. Red seemed like the best choice. So did green. But there was also yellow, orange, blue, and purple. I couldn't decide. I tested the red bow in the top corner. It looked nice. I added orange next to it. Then yellow followed by the rest of the colours. The top of the gift was covered in a rainbow.

"Grandma," I said. "Can I use six bows?"

She inspected my work then stuck a label on the side of the present with Grandpa's name.

"Yes, Jennifer," Grandma said, "you can use six bows."

I peeled the backing off the bows and made my rainbow. It was the first gift to go underneath the tree. When I asked Grandma where her presents were, she said she didn't want any, which I thought was strange because everyone wanted presents at Christmas.

Shortly after, Mom appeared from Grandpa's office and came into the living room. She sighed. "Vance won't give me the presents unless I come home."

Grandma turned to face my mother and pointed the scissors at her. "Don't you dare go back to that man, Brenda, so help me God."

I still couldn't understand what was so bad about him. I gave up wrapping presents and turned on the TV, hoping to drown my family out and find a Christmas movie. But I must've been too late because I found nothing but comedy shows, fast food commercials, and a news story about a Pan Am airplane crash.

My sister and I slept head-to-toe on the couch that night. Grandma's guinea pig mucked about in his cage, kicking up wood shavings, rattling the steel ball in his water bottle, and gnawing on the bars. I couldn't sleep either.

As I stared at the tree, I tried to figure out what Mom and Dad spoke about on the phone. I especially wondered why she was so upset when the answer to her problem seemed so easy to me: all we had to do was go home and then we'd get the presents. We would be a family again.

But if we didn't go home, then my father would have to bring the presents to my grandparents' after Christmas dinner, then take us home. Dad knew where my grandparents lived and he must've known we were there. I fell asleep not knowing if I'd get my home or my presents first, but I was sure Dad would come through because he wanted his family back just as much as I did. Then everyone would see how happy we actually were.

Grandma made my favourite breakfast: soft-boiled eggs served in little cups with toast points for dipping into the yolk. More presents had appeared underneath the tree overnight. Since the wrapping wasn't the same paper we had at home, I knew Dad hadn't stopped by. My sister and I no longer believed in Santa, which meant Grandma and Grandpa must have left them. Still, we couldn't wait to dig through them.

Grandpa joined us at the table with our mother while Grandma tidied up. He stared at his food and said nothing.

"What's the matter, Walt?" said Grandma.

He tapped a teaspoon on the side of one of the porcelain cups. "It's uncooked," he said. "The white is runny."

I tapped the side of my egg cup. The watery white mixed into the yolk and jiggled like Jell-O. It seemed no different than usual. Grandma said it was just water and told him to eat his breakfast, but Grandpa continued to stare at his plate. The longer he looked at it the more I wondered if I had eaten undercooked eggs.

My grandfather's silence unnerved me. I wanted to know what he was thinking so I knew how to feel. He seemed calm but not in the same way my father stayed calm when my mother messed up.

Once Mom bleached Dad's entire supply of welding coveralls in the laundry. Instead of yelling, he got down to her level, widened his eyes, and spoke to her very slowly. He reminded me of a kindergarten teacher showing a student how to behave. I thought he sounded friendly but for some reason Mom got all worked up and started yelling at him. Then he'd called her crazy, or a wingnut, and told her to stay away from his laundry.

I waited for Grandpa to talk to my grandmother the same slow, calm way but he didn't. Instead, he picked up a toast point and dipped it into the yolk. Grandma watched, her eyes hard and focused. I thought maybe he didn't want to upset her. Neither did I. So when he took a bite, I did too.

After breakfast, I dug under the tree and pulled out two boxes with my name on them. Both were from my grandparents. I ripped open the first one and found a shoebox. I lifted the lid and pulled back the tissue paper, hoping to find a small toy inside. But they were shoes.

I held up a pair of light pink lace-up shoes with the tiniest heel to show my mother. Grandma said I was growing up and that it was about time I wore shoes with heels. They were cute but not at all what I'd put on my wish list. I slid the shoes under the couch when no one was looking.

I wanted the Cabbage Patch Doll and Barbie waiting for me underneath the tree at home. I knew what they were by the shapes of the boxes. I knew in my heart there was still time for Dad to deliver them.

I tore open the second gift and pulled out a light-blue jean purse with a long, skinny shoulder strap filled with tissue paper.

"Every girl your age needs a purse," said Grandma.

I didn't know any girls in my class who had a purse. I didn't even have anything to put in it. I tucked it away with the shoes and mumbled a thank you.

Grandma handed Grandpa his gifts. When she set them on his lap, his face fell just as it had at breakfast. "What's all this, June?"

She told him to be quiet and just open his presents. She looked around the tree, underneath the skirt, and even in the branches. "Where's mine?"

"You said not to get you anything."

"Not even a bottle of perfume?"

Grandpa looked bored—like he'd gone inside his head—and I thought Grandma would cry. Instead, she stomped down the hall, each step heavier and angrier than the one before it. She slammed her bedroom door. "I didn't even get a bottle of smellies!"

Grandpa got up and rubbed his forehead.

"Dearie, please . . ." he called after her.

Grandma yelled that she wasn't making Christmas dinner for anyone.

I'd seen Grandma angry before. She'd kicked me out of rooms, out of her trailer, and even told me to get out of her hair. But I'd never seen her storm down a hall and slam a door behind her. This was a whole new Grandma and I didn't like it. I promised myself to be good in any way I could.

Mom sat with her unopened presents on her lap and said nothing. Did she get our grandmother anything? And if so, was it at home with ours? Maybe Dad would deliver it with ours so Grandma could get a present, too. Then maybe she'd finally come out of her room and we'd celebrate the holidays as we always had: we'd have a big homemade dinner, everyone would open presents, and then we'd all hug and kiss and, as usual, take forever to say goodbye when it was time to leave. All we needed was for my father to show up and my grandmother to come out of her room.

My grandfather eventually talked her into joining us. Mom helped Grandma peel carrots and potatoes at the kitchen sink before going back to her room. I thought maybe she'd call my father and invite him over for dinner but she told me to leave her alone because she was tired and needed a nap.

Grandma seasoned the turkey and prepared the stuffing while Mom went into her room to rest. Stephanie sat in front of the TV and watched Christmas shows. I had no interest in joining her. I waited on the couch by the living room window. Dad would come.

Later that afternoon, Mom emerged from her room. We ate dinner at the kitchen table in silence. Only the sound of forks and knives scraping plates and country music on the radio broke it. I ate everything on my plate, including the turkey, because I didn't want my grandmother to go back to her room again. But no matter how quiet I was, or how good I was, nothing erased the permanent frown from her face.

Grandma did the dishes alone that night. I fed leftover celery leaves to her guinea pig. After Grandma dried the last pot, she set it down with a heavy thud.

"Well," she sighed. "That's it. Christmas is over."

I didn't want to be ungrateful, but this was the worst Christmas ever. There was nothing I could have done to save it. I accepted gifts I didn't ask for, ate food I didn't enjoy, and wasted my time waiting for someone who never arrived. Grandma was right. Christmas was over. And with that, I officially stopped waiting for my dad.

Back at the shelter, Stephanie and I explored the whole place. Mom was out again and the workers were busy so we could go pretty much anywhere. We looked through a glass door into a library on the main floor with a wall-length bookshelf and a cozy armchair for reading. On top of the heavy wooden desk by the window sat a beige rotary phone, similar to the one at home.

I wasn't sure if we were allowed in because someone had closed the door. I tried the crystal knobs anyway. It was unlocked. I let myself in. I had a plan. Stephanie followed behind me. The library was by far the warmest and sunniest room in the house. The yellow walls and lace curtains made it nicer than the other rooms.

My sister searched the shelves for a kids' book. I snooped through the desk. Most of the stuff was boring: pens, pencils, and paperwork. But the phone captured and held my attention. I glanced over my shoulder at the glass doors and listened for voices nearby. None. I picked up the receiver.

Dad answered on the second ring. He asked where I was and I said at a women's shelter. He asked who drove us there and I said our neighbour. I asked what he did for Christmas.

He said, "Nothing." Dad asked where my mother was.

I said she was out but I didn't know where. I told him she went out a lot. He wanted to know who she was with. I said I didn't know.

My father asked for the shelter's address. I told him I didn't know that either. So he had me look out the window and describe what I saw. I mentioned the driveway and the side of someone else's house. Then I remembered the view from my bedroom: the city below, a traffic light at the bottom of the hill, and an orange bridge off in the distance.

Dad said he had to go. He asked for the phone number so he could talk to me again. So I read out the number written on the phone then hung up feeling good about myself.

My father called the shelter repeatedly each day—but not for me. He demanded to talk to my mother who was never there. The staff eventually made Mom call him back just to get him to stop. No one asked me how he got the phone number and I knew better than to tell. Dad told Mom it was only a matter of time before he found her, which terrified me.

The shelter separated my sister and me from our mother three days after Christmas—exactly one week after we'd arrived. They moved Mom down to the hall to a bedroom with hardwood floors. Stephanie and I ended up in a room with blue walls and bunk beds, but the excitement around the top bunk had already worn off.

Mom spent even less time at the shelter after the move.

But one afternoon, she sat us on her bed. I was so mad they put her in a room with ugly orange walls but she was smiling for the first time since we'd left home.

Mom said she'd met a very special man.

"Rob," I said.

"Yes."

Rob was so rich that he had an inground swimming pool with a diving board in his backyard. I didn't know what she meant by 'special.' If we were good, Mom continued, then he'd let us swim in it this summer.

She also explained it was important to be polite because Rob was her new boyfriend and we'd be meeting him soon. Then she had me hold out my hand. "I want you to say, 'Hello, Rob. My name is Jennifer. It's very nice to meet you.'"

By this time, I'd given up any hope that my family would get back together. My dad still refused to give up our Christmas presents and I suspected Mom wanted out of the shelter just as much as I did.

I imagined an underground swimming pool in our very own backyard, much better than the plastic kiddie pool we had at home. I could have all my old friends over. We could have a campout and swim underneath the stars. I couldn't wait for summer.

I held out my hand to my mother and said, "Hello, Rob. My name is Jennifer and it's very nice to meet you."

Aiden

COURTNEY RACICOT

"I must be some kind of masochist," was the only thought I could muster as I weaved through the throngs of holiday shoppers on my way back to work. With only three days left before Christmas, shoppers were panicked as they tried to cross names off their lists. Michael Bublé's Christmas CD seemed to be on repeat in every store in the mall. And it was only getting more challenging to keep a store looking full and fresh as the seasonal merchandise dwindled. Holiday seasons were beyond stressful for any person working retail. At that point in the year, I regularly questioned my sanity in choosing this career path. The past couple of months had already proven to be unbearable. In fact, the holiday stress that year had been downright suffocating as my husband, Rory, and I dealt with the grief of being without Aiden. Despite having only been parents for a little less than a year, we couldn't remember how to be childless.

Aiden had come into our lives as abruptly as he had left it. We had spent two years trying for a child. For two years, I ached as my Facebook feed was infiltrated with ultrasound photos and my friends' swelling bellies while I tossed negative pregnancy tests into the trash every month. I cooed wistfully whenever a mother came into the store with her baby. After two full years of trying to conceive, Rory and I found ourselves driving by the Children's Aid Society building. We looked at each other, and without speaking, without hesitating, we pulled into the parking lot and chose public adoption. We introduced ourselves at reception. We asked for some brochures, but the enthusiastic receptionist quickly summoned a social worker named Laura to speak with us. Within fifteen minutes, we'd begun our adoption profile.

I tried to memorize the moment as we exited the building after that first meeting. The sun was shining, and my husband and I giddily snuck glances at each other like we had a secret. We were on an entirely new path, and it felt right.

We only became more sure of our decision at each phase of the process. We attended the mandatory adoption classes and allowed Laura to infiltrate every part of our lives in the name of a 'home study.' She interrogated us about everything from our parenting beliefs to our drinking habits and relationships with our own parents. At the same time, she walked through our home, checking for safe railings and socket covers. It was invasive, but we persevered, steadfast in our certainty that we were doing the right thing.

Seven months later, validation came in the best form.

Aiden was six months old, cherub-cheeked, and he turned our worlds upside down. With less than twenty-four hours' notice that we would be parents, it was a flip of reality. One day, we were planning late-night appetizer dates and holidays to Vegas; the next, we were filling two carts at Babies R Us and debating if a baby wipes warmer was essential.

The transition phase was hectic. We spent a week with Aiden's current foster family to bridge the transition. As first-time parents, it was like a baby boot camp. We learned everything from bathing to preparing formula. We developed faster reflexes for things such as grabbing a cloth before Aiden spit up all over our clothes or getting the clean diaper on before being peed on. Aiden's foster mother, Melanie, was patient and kind as she gradually handed over care.

During Aiden's nap times, she would bring us plates of food, and we would talk. Melanie had spent substantial time with Aiden's birth mother in the early weeks of his life, and she filled us in on the history. Amber was sixteen years old, had dropped out of school, and lived in a tent with her abusive boyfriend, Cody. With no care plan for Aiden, he was apprehended at the hospital and had been living with Melanie and her family ever since. Amber had not shown up for the majority of her scheduled visits with Aiden and hadn't seen him at all in over two months, resulting in the Society's decision to find him an adoptive home.

AIDEN

*

Aiden moved into our home officially less than two weeks after we received the call from the Children's Aid Society. He was everything that parents dream of in a baby. He was happy, healthy, and adorable. We immediately fell in love with him and strived to be the parents we felt he deserved. Rory and I researched all the best foods to introduce, making our own baby foods. We took him to parks, pushing him gently in the baby swings. We went to playgroups and continued to visit with Melanie and her family. If Aiden was fussy, we would take turns soothing him by dancing around the living room with him to Mumford and Sons' "I Will Wait For You." I fell more in love with my husband as I watched him bathe our baby every night, counting his toes and singing him songs. The most peace I had ever felt came when I would cradle Aiden close to me in a darkened room while bottle-feeding him before bedtime.

Two months after Aiden's move into our home, just as we had settled into our new routines and my husband had returned to work, the phone call came.

It was Laura. She told me Aiden's birth mother, Amber, had come out of the woodwork and wanted to pursue reunification. She told me how Amber was taking steps to establish a care plan for Aiden. She told me about Amber's resilience and how much she had overcome. And I believed her. But I could only tell her about the unwavering love I

now felt for Aiden, and that Rory and I had committed ourselves to make sure Aiden had the best life possible. It did
not include Amber's return.

The rose-coloured glasses came off quickly as we realized
how naive we were about the child welfare system. We had
no idea the roller coaster we were signing up for when we
took in our little munchkin. Contrary to our initial understanding of the situation, Aiden was not adoptable.

There was no time for the shock to set in; suddenly, we
were navigating a complex schedule comprised of visitations,
court dates, teen parenting classes, and social worker meetings. Amber was suddenly not only present but an active
participant in Aiden's life. At the same time, she crossed
items off the list of tasks the judge requested of her for the
courts to consider reunification. Although still struggling,
she moved back into her grandmother's home, finished her
high-school courses, and maintained regular hours at her
job at a local fast food joint. She was suddenly attending
every scheduled visitation. At the agency's request, we kept
a correspondence book between ourselves and Amber; it
travelled in the diaper bag to and from Aiden's visits with
Amber. As the weeks passed, and Amber grew more confident, I would retrieve the book from the bag only to read
notes asking me to stop allowing Aiden to call me "Mama"

and asking us to adjust his nap schedule. We struggled with Aiden's vacillation between tantrums and exhaustion as his schedule was regularly disrupted by increased visitation or a sudden teen parenting assessment to attend.

Meanwhile, the agency reneged on its agreement to support us and moved us from the Adoption Department to the Foster Parent Department. Full of panic about the uncertainty of our child's future should he be returned to his birth mother, we scrutinized Amber's social media, reporting any contact with the birth father, from whom she claimed to be separated. We kept charts of Aiden's behaviours when his schedule was disrupted and notes of when Amber ignored his strict lactose-free diet. We grilled the social workers about their impressions of the visits, honing in on any potentially disturbing details. There were many opportunities for this; social workers visited us at least a half dozen times a month.

About six months in, Rory and I attended a monthly 'all-team' meeting at the Society. All the social workers involved in Aiden's case, the managers and sometimes consultants would participate. At this session, the assessor from the Teen Parenting Skills workshops, which Amber and Aiden had been attending, was present. When given her time to present, the assessor reported that Amber was making excellent progress and seemed to be starting to bond with Aiden.

"I think she can do this!" she said excitedly at the end of her speech.

I stormed out. Rory followed me into a secluded stairwell and held me as I cried. I could feel his face wet against my cheek.

Laura found us in the stairwell a short while later. "The Society realizes how difficult and complicated this situation has become. We want to pay for you to go to counselling." Within days, we were scheduling weekly therapy sessions into our already busy lives.

At the recommendation of Aiden's lawyer, we hired our own lawyer and explored all options to keep our child. It was only becoming clearer the direction this situation was heading. Aiden was only getting older the longer this was dragged out in court. Right before Aiden turned eighteen months, we met with all of the social workers involved in his case. The decision was made to return Aiden to his birth mother the following week. Devastation, as we had never known, settled over our lives.

I blacked out after they took Aiden from me for the final time. My brother put away all the toys and baby items in the nursery, a shrine to the son we couldn't keep. It would remain that way for a long time.

Gradually, life returned to us, more out of necessity than

desire. Our family returned to their own homes, friends stopped checking in every day, and eventually we returned to work. But a full recovery seemed impossible. Halloween passed, Aiden's birthday approached, and a friend fell pregnant again. Whenever Rory and I felt we were moving forward, another event pushed us back into the tides of grief. It felt like there had been an invisible cap to our joy, and we had reached it before Aiden had even reached his second birthday. It was all we could do to put one foot in front of the other and get through each day.

Therefore, that holiday season, I went to work each day with a bitter heart, throwing myself into providing the best holiday shopping experience to our shoppers in an effort to distract myself. Mourning was a luxury reserved for the upper class. I walled myself off from any triggers—I avoided the mall hallways, where I could see mothers gleefully setting up their children on Santa's lap. But that morning, I had left in a hurry while on a conference call and had forgotten my lunch on the counter, necessitating a run to the food court.

On my way back to work, I passed Santa's workshop in the centre court and caught a glimpse of her. Amber. Her uncle stood beside her, holding Aiden in his arms. They were looking at pictures on the photographer's computer. My heart stopped, and I froze in place. Her blue eyes, so much like his, turned and locked with mine. Last year I was one of those mothers setting up my child for the perfect Santa Claus picture. I had dressed Aiden in little Gap overalls and a classic Hudson's Bay cardigan. Other mothers commented on what a cute baby he was, and I smiled back modestly. It felt odd receiving that compliment when I hadn't birthed him myself. I held his favourite stuffed elephant at eye level to make him smile. And when we finally got the shot, I picked up my baby and thanked Santa. I bundled Aiden in the stroller and waited for the assistant to print our photos.

It had been then, in the middle of the mall, that I spotted a young man staring at us from fifteen feet away. I froze with recognition. We had never met, but I knew his face from a picture I kept in Aiden's keepsake box. I had memorized that face as I searched the photo for similarities. This was Aiden's birth father. Cody. The Children's Aid Society had not permitted him visits nor allowed us to meet him due to safety concerns. They told us he was potentially dangerous. My throat tightened as I wondered if he was actually recognizing Aiden or if it was my imagination. After all, he hadn't seen Aiden in more than four months. But I knew Amber posted photos of Aiden on Facebook occasionally; Cody possibly had seen them.

Cody approached us, and I knew there was no escaping.

"That's my son," he said, pointing to Aiden, staring curiously from the stroller.

I had a millisecond to make a decision. I could say that CAS wouldn't want this, that he could call the lawyer if he wanted to see him. But I watched the tenderness on Cody's face as he stared at Aiden. Cody was young himself, not yet eighteen. I took a breath, steadied myself and held out my hand.

"You must be Cody," I smiled as he tentatively took my hand and shook. "I'm Courtney. How are you?"

"Okay . . ." He could barely look away from Aiden, as if his eyes were hungry and would never fill of him. "He looks good."

I smiled as warmly as I could manage. "He is good. He's very smart for his age; he's walking and talking already. And we just got his Santa Claus pictures done." I pulled out the envelope the photographer had just handed to me. The photos were still warm. Cody flipped through them, smiling ruefully.

"Would you like one?" I asked. He replied that he would love one to show his grandmother. I took the two 5x7s and handed them to him.

"Both? Really?" He looked surprised as I nodded. It wasn't a problem at all. I was just grateful for how well this was going.

"Can I kiss him?" Cody asked tentatively. I nodded, even though he reeked of cigarettes, and I was sure that our social workers would disapprove. But Aiden was good-natured and smiled. Cody patted his hair. "His hair is so long. Don't cut it."

I smiled back. "I like it too; he looks like a blond Beatle."

As he went to turn away, Cody paused. "Please take care of him."

It was my turn to be surprised, but I nodded and replied, "Of course."

Like that day nearly one year ago, my mind couldn't decide how to react. But my body seemed to know what to do, and I slowly walked towards Amber. She turned to say something to her uncle, who stepped a few feet away with Aiden as I came face-to-face with her. The last time I'd seen her, I was in a courtroom asking for custody of her son.

"I'm sorry, I just couldn't walk away without at least wishing you guys a Merry Christmas," I said. And just as I had to decide how to handle my interaction with Cody last Christmas, Amber now had the decision to make.

Amber held out her arms for a hug, and I hugged her tightly, sincerely. At that moment, I realized we were the same. She had fought for her son, and she had won. She had done exactly what I had done, and the details didn't matter now. My resentment couldn't rest with her. This young woman, desperate for her son, had struggled out of an abusive relationship and challenging circumstances and reinvented her life. When she realized she was losing him, she did everything the courts asked of her to get Aiden back. It was nothing less than what we had done for Aiden.

"I'm very proud of you," I told her quietly.

I wondered why I chose those words, but a second later, I realized it was because it was the truth. I was proud that my son's birth mother had come up against all odds and turned her life around for him. It was not the life I would have chosen for him; they would have their own struggles. But she had strength and character and love. It may just be enough.

"Would you like to see Aiden?" she asked. I met her eyes and understood that this was her gift to me.

"Yes," I said softly. She turned to her uncle and took Aiden, and oh! Suddenly he was in my arms. I could understand now how Cody could not look away from him. I could look at Aiden forever as he stared back at me, taking me in. It had been seven months since I had last seen him. He stared at me curiously, with a flicker of recognition, but he couldn't quite place me. My heart broke, although I knew it was better that he didn't recognize me. I held my breath briefly, determined not to sob as a few tears escaped me.

"You're so big now!" I said. "Big boy!" Aiden smiled and patted my cheek with one chubby hand. I kissed his hand and handed him back to Amber. My heart ached with the motion. Then he grabbed her hair and said, "Mama."

"That's right," I said to him. "That's your Mama." And I tried not to think of how he called me "mamamamama" every morning from his crib.

Amber smiled. "It's all okay." I wasn't sure if she was reassuring me or talking to her uncle. I smiled anyway. With a deep breath, I took comfort in knowing he was surrounded by love and hope.

"Of course."

After wishing each other Merry Christmas, we parted ways, and I walked back to my store in a daze. I let the tears fall in the quiet of the stockroom, surrounded by leftover garland and denim. I sobbed full-on into a knit Christmas sweater.

It took me a moment to realize that my tears were more than tears of grief. I now recognized that our chance meeting was what I had been waiting for—to see, with my own eyes, that Aiden was safe and Aiden was loved.

My tears were tears of relief.

I paused for a moment and wiped my face on the argyle sleeve of the sweater I'd been holding. I pulled out my cell phone and sent a text to Rory:

We are all going to be okay.

Coyote's Tail

JOSEPH KAKWINOKANASUM

With Christmas just days away, we had no tree, no decorations to mark the season, and no word from Mom or her boyfriend Ed. They were on a bender. But if Mom were here, she'd have insisted on putting up stuff the first week of December, and they would have stayed up until the end of Ukrainian Christmas in January.

The usual decorations would have included tinsel strung along the whole perimeter of the living room and dining room and, if she had enough, she would have ordered us to do the same in the kitchen. She would have also made us set up a tree in the corner by the big window.

It was never anything special. If I went to my friend's house, I'd see the same ornaments. But it was special to Mom. This was part of the veil to hide our poverty. I felt it was a diversion to give the nosey neighbours the impression we were okay. At Christmas, she dressed the house like she dressed her children. We had specific clothes we were allowed to wear with her in public. It was a reflection of her ability to raise her children. Even as a ten-year-old, all of it pissed me off. But Mom was gone. And my brothers, sisters, and I weren't invested in decorating the house. Who could blame us?

I remember sitting in the bare living room with the cat on my lap. Minosis. (He was a fantastic pet. When my brother came home with him as a kitten, arguments ensued over what to name the poor creature. Mom yelled, "Enough! Its name is Minosis." It was the Cree word for kitten and that was the end of it.) Everything in the room was beat-up, well-worn, with blankets and Afghans covering stains and tattered armrests. I thought about how I was sick and tired of explaining my poverty. In past Christmases, I had to find ways to tell my teachers, again, why I didn't really do the holiday.

For example, the year before, after the winter break, all the kids were talking about what Santa had brought them.

I had to lie about what I received. I told people I got clothes. Because it was boring, and they'd leave me alone. I became the equivalent of the wallflower at a dance, I was passed over, ignored, and that was fine with me.

It got worse. Our teacher asked us to write a few paragraphs about how we *felt* about the gifts we received. He then sent us home that day with a note to our parents stating that it would be a nice gesture if we all donated one toy each to the poor. I failed this project. "It will reflect on your overall grade," my teacher told me.

It was always like that. Every holiday, I had to exclude myself from any school program that required parental approval or money. I always had to say no to class trips. Eventually my teachers would stop asking me for any sort of donations. But that day hadn't come yet.

I was a ten-year-old confronting the bare walls, the missing tree. The cat's claws dug through my thin denim pants. I knew I still had to lie. Sure, lying made me a liar, and lying was bad. But trying to explain why we didn't have a tree would be harder. I've always understood why Mom liked to keep up appearances, to look like we were a normal family. We couldn't be six kids dependent on an undependable and her boyfriend, who most days were partying at the Park Hotel in Dawson Creek. We all knew welfare was a risk. The authorities could take us away. The threat was the government. That's what made me a liar. It forced me to fabricate how turkey and gravy tasted. It forced me to dream up presents under the tree.

The more I thought about it, the angrier I became. Indignant as I was, I understood that finding a tree for our living room was easier than explaining to my classmates why we didn't have one. In a small village like Pouce, everyone's business is everyone's business, and the local rumour mill was unforgiving of non-Christians. God, I hated Christmas, but like it or not, I knew what I had to do.

I picked myself up off the couch. At least I could enjoy some of the sunshine outside. The cat looked at me with its eyes half-closed, as if he had heard my thoughts.

I went downstairs. I picked up my .22 cal, sleeved it into a big leather sling case. I threw in a box of short shells and the binoculars that I had traded some bike parts I found at the dump for. I put on my winter gear: thermal underwear, wool socks, undershirt, and leggings. Over that, I layered my parka and snow pants. I grabbed one pair of moose-hide mittens, a wool scarf, and a toque. If there was one thing that growing up here taught me it was this: I hate being cold.

As I sat down to tie my boots, and by this time I was sweating, it occurred to me that I had received a gift once. It was a shovel. I was four. My mother's boyfriend at the time, not Ed, said, "Now you don't have a reason to not shovel the walk." So I did. I shovelled our own, and that particular Christmas morning, one of Mom's drinking buddies was so impressed by my efforts that he took me aside and said, "There's money in that shovel. A valuable gift it is."

He gave me a brand new two-dollar bill, patted me on the back and returned to Mom's party. I was spellbound and my jaw dropped at the notion. Later that morning, I tugged on the guy's sleeve. He bent to my level.

"How do I make more money with this?" I held up the shovel.

The man pointed out the window. "There's lots of walks out there need shov'lin'."

My mother gave me an approving look. The man said, "You walk up to the door and ask if they'd like their walk shovelled. Five bucks a drive, two for the walk." He stood, smiled, and his blue eyes shone like wet glass. I absorbed it. I did that.

I worked that shovel to the death. Literally. I broke the handle by lunch. It was a cheap piece of shit, but I made a few bucks with it. Not a bad Christmas. I was like that around a lot of the men in Mom's life. Some encouraged me to be self-reliant. Like my uncle Angus. He was a couple years younger than Mom. As rare as it was to visit him, I remember every time I spent with him. Uncle was gentle, kind, told great stories and had a huge, infectious laugh. Plus he always had money in his wallet. He encouraged me to work hard, to be proud of myself, to do what I had to do.

I opened the door and stepped out. The air was cold and dry. I felt the skin around my mouth and nose instantly react to the freezing cold.

The wood stairs creaked as I made my way down. The snow crackled and squeaked, and drifts in some places were three or more metres high against the house and buried the two-metre fence. Only the tops of the posts poked through.

From the backyard shed, I grabbed the old beat-up

wooden toboggan that someone in the family had found abandoned years ago. I inspected the contents of my back-pack: one safety kit, a length of nylon rope, dried meat and a dehydrated apple, enough for three days if I conserved; dried kindling, an old newspaper, matches, and enough wood to start a small fire. I added a collapsible bow saw and a folding shovel I'd bought at a church rummage sale for a buck-fifty, and finally a litre of water in a glass Coke bottle. Before school closed for winter break, I had signed out a pair of snowshoes from the gym supplies room. I strapped them to the backpack with an old shoelace.

I was all set. I trudged my way towards the edge of the village.

I weaved my way that morning through a winter won-derland. I passed between the Andersons' and the Apiwins' homes. In Cree, *apiwin* sort of means 'house,' but literally, it means 'tepee.' As I walked the waist-deep paths trenched between the houses, I felt the crunch of snow under my feet. Atop the homes, snow cornices hung over the eavestroughs. Wreaths hung on the doors and, visible through the windows, decorations hung on walls, and trees were festooned with garland, and lights, and no doubt had presents under them.

I continued past the Blue Bird Hotel, where some of the regular folks usually kept a few bottles aside for me to return for the deposit. I walked on the road because sidewalks were an afterthought in the village's design. It took about twelve minutes to reach the other side of town. I could see the ramshackle Canadian Legion, an old broken-down hangout for the old soldiers from the First, Second, Korean and, most recent, Vietnam Wars. Sometimes on lazy Sundays, me and a couple of buddies hung out with them and listened to old war stories, then we would go out and play war games.

Normally, because of my mom, I didn't like establishments where adults gathered to drink. But the Legion, where all the local socials were held, provided villagers with a place to gather. The events were always great fun, and they offered the main attraction of giving away all the free pop a kid could want.

The Legion was always open, even if you just needed to warm your hands up from the cold. I popped my head in through the door to see if there was anything going on. Nothing but staff and war vets drinking coffee, smoking cigarettes, and reminiscing. One of the old Native ladies offered me a coffee and I accepted. I loaded it with white sugar and powdered milk. The warmth in my belly. I felt a surge of energy as the sugar hit hard. The Native lady smiled and waved as I put my cup in a dish bin.

I followed a path behind the Legion south into the pines, where I knew, from all of my walks and adventures, that there were Christmas trees. I headed for the sleigh hills where kids made a day out of whipping down several different runs. For me, it was a convenient way down to the trailhead. There was one run aptly called Daredevil, pure vertical madness marked by two huge slumps in the topography. Another slide, dangerously close to Daredevil, was in the shape of a lazy C. It was crazy fast. One wrong turn or a little slip and you'd wind up on your way to the brambles and a broken tailbone, but if you negotiated the hazard around a hard-right berm it was a straight stretch for some two hundred metres, pocked with the occasional little jump and dip that would send you flying if you didn't expect it. Do this and you were an instant legend.

From a distance I could see kids gathered around a small fire. The cries of joy and laughter. I settled onto the old toboggan. The rusted wood screws and rope that held her together allowed me to flex it in a way that I could steer it somewhat. It was a slow start at first, but about ten metres into the ride my speed had tripled; I approached the first bend fast and, as I yanked the rope to the right and shifted my weight, the old toboggan carved the icy path. The rest of the ride was a straight, bumpy blur over the little jumps and dips. It would have been nice to forget Christmas altogether and just ride down those runs all day.

At the bottom of the hill, I steered clear of the kids

gathered around the fire. They talked loudly over one another about the much anticipated day. Smoke billowed from the fire and curled towards town on a light breeze over the treetops. As I had nothing good to add to the conversation, I avoided the buzz and excited discussions. Lying about what I was expecting for Christmas would have nauseated me. I stayed focused on finding a tree.

I pulled my toboggan behind me and stopped near the kids to put on the snowshoes. A couple of school friends were there, and I noted a few of the village bullies. I made as little a scene as possible. People around here talked, and I didn't want anyone to know what I was doing and what we couldn't afford.

I said hi, exchanged a few jokes with them without drawing attention, then headed towards the creek. From there I followed a trail I knew well. The path was narrow, and as I walked, I recognized the tracks of many snowshoe rabbits, and small claw marks in the snow made by various birds scrounging for food. I felt sorry for the poor creatures. I saw huge ravens puffed up in their winter plumage high in the treetops, who sounded off as I passed, as if to warn the wilderness: something wicked this way comes.

The sun was high now, but the clear blue sky had shifted to overcast. For some reason I found myself staring up at it and that made my eyes water. I stopped after about half a kilometre to get my bearings. Sound travelled fast and far through the cold air, and I could still hear the kids playing on the slopes.

The weather was going to change.

I looked back to where I came from, inspected the cloud cover, and slowly breathed in deep. The air smelled like snow. I could taste the crispness of frozen moisture carried from the west. It blew over the foothills into the basin of the South Peace region. The result was a thick blanket of snow, and when the freshet came, torrents of water filled basins, and roared down river beds and deep ditches. Floods were common in the spring.

I surveyed the spindly trees around me, and nothing stood out as a good candidate. I knew I needed to be quick with this tree thing, but I couldn't have just any tree. I would need to walk deeper into the forest where the smaller trees were protected from the constant winds. I moved south along the trail for another half hour and forked west from the main trail. Out that way was a stand of trees that looked healthy and strong. The land was flat and forgiving and perfect for my footwear. I walked an hour on this path. I figured it was about two o'clock. The sun would be down in a couple of hours. I was okay with the elements, I was even okay with the approaching darkness, but the notion of running into anything larger than a fox stuck in the front of my mind like a roadblock. I would have to be cautious and keep ultra-alert for any signs of danger.

Ice crystals formed in the air and the overcast sank into a low cloud cover, and the temperature increased to what felt like a balmy minus twenty or so, which sounds nice but I knew what was coming. All I could do was stop for a break, snack on a bit of dried meat, and take a sip of water. I looked up again. I could see definition in the looming clouds. But there was no snow, not yet.

I finished my meat and continued through a small stand where the deciduous trees gave way to conifers. At that moment, I felt I was being stalked by the weather—another roadblock—and it took all my mental energy to put it to the back of my mind. I reminded myself that whatever happened, I had planned for the worst. With the snowshoes, I would make good time. Anyhow, I was going into the thick forest and it would shelter me from the elements, and that brought me some relief.

The deeper I went, the more I found tracks of deer, fox, coyote, moose, wolf, and the odd cougar track. I feared the wolf pack most. I looked behind me regularly. Out here I was easy prey.

The time, the weather, the sense of being watched made me hurry. I breathed with a rhythm; I quickened my pace, half walking, half jogging. I figured there was only one hour left of regular light and maybe a half-hour of dusk, and then it would be pitch black.

I emerged from the forest and into a clearing. High above, a raven soared in my direction, the silhouette of its tailfeathers flared open, and its wide wings flapped almost sideways as its claws grasped the top of an ancient pine tree. It let out a deep call that sounded slightly muffled. I strained my ears, closed my eyes, focused on the noises around me, and realized I could only hear the forest sounds. The deeper into the forest I went, I started assessing prospective Christmas trees. "Too short, too tall, no, not the pine, I want a spruce." I liked the smell and lushness of the white spruce tree; besides, the pines were too spindly and balsam fir made me itchy.

The air went still. My breath hung momentarily like a cloud in front of me, only to crystallize and fall like snow. I looked up. The cloud cover was even thicker and lower than before. Snow began to fall. It started light and, second by second, the flakes got larger. I was in trouble.

Time was not on my side, so I decided to find shelter.

I backtracked as far as the snow allowed. I followed my own footprints for about half an hour until the snow, now coming down heavily, finally covered them. The thick and heavy snow meant there were huge, near mountainous, tree wells. It was my best choice for a shelter.

I found a large hemlock tree, where I knocked all my

stuff off the toboggan and stood it up like a candy cane. I didn't want to lose it in the snow. I unlaced my snowshoes and planted them vertically beside the toboggan, too. I climbed up the snow and ice of the well. It was tricky, but finally made it to where the lowest boughs of the hemlock tree ended. About a foot of space existed between the bottom branches and the crest of the tree well. I peeked inside. It was clear. I slipped off my backpack and pulled out the rope. I tied one end to one of the thicker boughs and straddled the crest of the tree well. The bare ground was four metres below.

I re-slung my backpack over my shoulders and eased myself down. It was slightly warmer at the bottom of the well, but I quickly realized I was not the only one who had been here. I caught a slight whiff of a wild animal—I recognized the odour from a hunting trip in the fall. It smelled of a buck, like the deer we'd killed and skinned. Such a distinctive scent.

I felt for my safety kit at the bottom of my pack and, inside that, found a small flashlight. I beamed it around. A bed of fine hair or fur covered the ground. I looked closer, picked up a tuft, held it to my nose. It was deer hair. I sighed with relief. I made my way around the trunk of the tree, and there were dry needles and bits of sticks and twigs. I pulled out my shovel and dug a small pit. I lit some small emergency candles from the safety kit to save the batteries in my flashlight. I collected enough pieces of the dry ground cover and combined it with the dry wood and paper I brought. I wanted to make a fire big enough to keep wild things away and small enough not to burn me out of my shelter.

I had no idea how long I was going to be there, so I settled in. Inside the tree well, it was still cold but I was dry and out of the wind.

The soft yellow light shed by the fire created shadows. Shapes reflected off the icy wall of the tree well. To keep busy and avoid thinking about my isolation and the gravity of the situation, I pulled out my knife and carved the date, year, and my initials into the trunk of the tree. I worked slowly, but it still took me less than an hour.

I removed the shovel from my bag and unfolded it, securing the blade with a metal collar at the base of the handle. The shovel worked great through the thick ice; the snow underneath had an icy, granular texture, but it was compacted. I could carve out footholds to climb up to the top of the tree well. Not that there was much to see. This time of year in these parts nights are long. The sunset was about four-thirty and sunrise was nine-thirty, quarter-to-ten. I had about fifteen hours of darkness to get through before I could make my way back home.

"I'll be damned if I am going to stay here for the whole night," I said out loud in defiance. There was nowhere for the sound of my voice to go. I decided to make my way back home when the snow stopped.

I prepared an area where I could lie and wait. I snapped a small dry branch and began to whittle away the time. I thought about the last time I saw Uncle Angus. Our family was vacationing on the reserve. Uncle Angus let me tag along with him on a business trip to Prince Albert. On the way a coyote streaked across the road and Uncle braked hard and swerved to miss it. It was mangy with a skinny body and a big incongruous fluffy tail. It made me laugh. Uncle asked, "Know how Coyote got his tail?"

I replied, "No."

"Well!" replied Uncle in his big voice, "Coyote used to look like Brother Wolf, noble and majestic. His coat was one of the finest of all Creation. A great mane and tail to match. One day Coyote and Raven were telling jokes and playing outside a small village when they noticed that the women going through their cycle, gathered in the same big tepee with their menstrual blood being carefully collected and stored in carved wooden bowls by the men outside the entrance of the tepee. The men took turns and waited on the women. They carried in food, water, extra blankets, and kept wood for the fire. The Coyote and Raven were smart, sly, and tricky as well. But Raven was a bit craftier and knew it was wrong to possess the menstrual blood.

"It was at that time that Raven noticed the men changing watches. Raven and Coyote could hear the prayers of the women inside the tepee. One man spoke and quietly gave an order for more water to another man. The man who stayed turned and stooped to check in on the women. The bowl of menstrual blood sat beside the entrance practically unguarded. It was at this moment that Raven noticed a window of opportunity, and was curious to see what might happen to Coyote if Raven convinced him to take the menstrual blood. What would the Creator think and, more curiously, what would the Creator do?

"Knowing the Creator had left explicit orders to never mess with powerful magic, Raven bet Coyote that he was not quick and quiet enough to even get close to stealing the sacred magic. Coyote, always eager to show off his skills and stealth, took the bet and Raven egged him on. Coyote snuck his way through the brush and into the tall grasses at the edge of the small village. Raven took a seat at the top of the tallest tree to have an unobstructed view. Coyote's tail poked up from the grass. He looked left and right, took one step, then two, then a full run to the back of the tepee unseen.

"Coyote could hear Raven's cawing and clicking and cheering him on. Coyote kept his belly close to the ground and ears perked way up, his eyes scanning the above for any sign of danger, nose sniffing the air. Coyote knew he was close to winning the bet and looked over his shoulder. Raven was flapping and hopping on his branch atop the village's tallest tree, urging Coyote on.

"Raven thought to himself that Coyote would never make it when the unthinkable happened. Raven saw Coyote whip around in a flash and grab the bowl and run back to the tall grass at the edge of the village. And just as Coyote took his first taste of the bowl's contents, Creator appeared in a flash of bright light, angry and disappointed. Coyote's punishment for his terrible act was to be turned from a majestic, beautiful creature to a mangy, scrawny mongrel. Creator left Coyote's tail as a reminder of what his coat used to look like. And furthermore, every coyote from that day on would bear the shame of their ancestor. And that is how Coyote got their tail."

I came to, like being slapped out of a good dream, suddenly missing my uncle. To this day, I can't tell you if I was the Coyote, the Raven, the coat or the tail. But I've never forgotten that story.

I climbed up the well to look outside. It was no longer pitch black. The moon was out. The snow had eased off and had covered everything up with a foot-high layer of fresh dry stuff. My tracks were now long gone, and the conifers, covered in the white stuff, resembled massive coyote's tails sticking straight up.

I wondered what was happening at home. Did my siblings have any idea I was even gone? I really don't know why I cared. The less I was in the way, the more I kept to myself and blended in, the more I fake-laughed at their racist Native jokes, the easier it was for me. I betrayed myself, felt that shame, and wondered if I had a tail, would it look like Coyote's, and would it just stay somewhere between my legs?

I secured my pack and left some dried fruit for the deer who gave up its home. I made a short prayer for good fortune and put out the fire.

I gave up trying to find a Christmas tree.

So, of course, as I made my way along the trail home, I noticed a small tree that would be perfect. As I approached it a wave of emotion came over me.

Cutting down the small sapling, a tree given to us by the Creator, for Christmas was wrong, especially after a tree like it had given me shelter from the cold and snow.

I kept walking. I left the tree to grow. A good feeling filled me. I'd saved a tree.

Uncle Angus once told me, "It's quite simply, my boy, that Natives didn't cut down a tree, make a cross out of it, and hang their Messiah on it to die. Christians kneel and pray for forgiveness for murder, for their savagery and for what they did. Natives pray standing up, hands held palms up to the heavens. We don't require forgiveness. It is that simple."

I continued down the trail towards home and random thoughts of good and bad fluttered through my head.

The moon was truly bright and when I looked up to the sky through the bony deciduous canopy, I noticed most of the clouds were now wisps. I could smell a campfire and hear the voices of people. I hid behind a tree, inspecting the scene, listening for friendly voices. I scanned the sleigh hill. As late as it was, there was still a large group of kids taking turns down the hill. Another string of children marched back up. I saw my two brothers and sister warming themselves by the fire. I was careful not to be seen.

As I approached our house, I saw the lights were on, smoke rising from the chimney. Christmas lights were strung around the roof. They shone through a blanket of snow. In the driveway was Mom's car, still warm. I peered through a frosted living room window. Ed was putting a star on a tree.

Carefully, I made my way around the back, pulling along my toboggan. I stored it in the shed and put the snowshoes and pack next to it. I climbed through the basement storage room window and eased my way down to the concrete floor.

I heard Elvis Presley's "Blue Christmas" playing upstairs. Mom and Ed funning about. Soft as a feather and quick as a jackrabbit, I snuck my way to my cot. I undressed, but kept on my long underwear, and slipped under the covers.

Vienna

JOANNA BAXTER

In early November, Mom calls me over to her house. I live nearby and she always calls me over whenever she needs help doing anything on the www. I swear the worst thing that ever happened to Mom was the extinction of the Yellow Pages. Every time she needs to find a phone number or an address, it's like she wakes from a normal, nice dream to find herself in an unfamiliar dystopia where paper doesn't exist. She's sitting there with one arthritic finger licked, ready to flick through those delicate ochre pages, only to find there's no big yellow book, there's no pages at all, and the only thing staring back at her is this sleek alien metal device with a perplexing glow-in-the-dark apple that might blow up if she tries to use it with a wet finger. So naturally, she rarely touches the thing because no one in their right mind wants an explosion. Sometimes I don't hold Mom's inability to adapt to the www against her. Sometimes I almost envy her ineptitude, despite the fact it means I have to go over there every time to reset her device just to get her back on the home page.

I get to her house as quick as I can because I'm sensitive to how the www activates her nerves. I feel that same stress when a password I've used forty times refuses to work or a form gets deleted after I've filled in the whole damn thing. My dad loved to say, "Don't let the turkeys get you down" and man, the www can be one hell of a turkey.

I can see how Mom's morale goes deep-six after the heartless computer taunts her all day long about how she's not sharp enough to remember the sequence of all fifteen symbols and numbers and capitals required to access her Netflix account. And then there's this circle-jerk helplessness she's honed, where she'll get a perfectly great idea that she can't execute because she doesn't dare blow anything up. So she suspends herself in that endless mid-arc of incomplete projects, a purgatory between thinking and doing. The www really is like her arch-enemy, blocking her before the finish line and eroding her confidence. Mom remains defiant with a quote that used to be cute but now just feels sad: "I'm high-touch, not high-tech." I can feel the edge of that abyss sometimes too.

I arrive to find Mom lying on the daybed. Instead of a regular hello, she says, "I have a terrible headache." This is her code for, "The turkeys have gotten me down," which is also her code for, "By-god-somebody-do-all-this-shit-for-me-now." I give my abilities a solid C+ when it comes to the www and attribute any remote talent on my part to the simple fact of being born at the tail end of the www generation. The least I can do for Mom is to Google something for her a couple of times per week. I'm not convinced that she even knows which symbols mean PLAY and STOP and PAUSE. I think she just fakes it, has been faking it since about 1981 by pushing buttons until something desirable happens. Mom thinks I'm some kind of www genius.

Mom's overwhelming idea is to buy some tickets for a concert, which is something that, like so many other things, can only be done via the www. Mom's almost eighty, and the mere mention of Christmas is like pouring gas on her undying Olympic flame of anxiety. One year she'll have a crazed Santa-load of presents for everyone, followed by the next where she'll exclaim that no one's getting anything and that she's flat-out boycotting the whole thing. I'm okay to tone down the over-the-top extravagance of gift-giving, and even the grandchildren have grown accustomed to her all-or-nothing approach. This year, she's determined to take my daughter and me to a choir, with a side note that this will be her Christmas present to us and to her, and that there will be nothing else. She makes this last part clear, really eyeballs it at me as if to preempt some spoiled, childish pouting on my behalf. As if I wasn't well-attuned to her annual wildcard swashbuckling attitude about holiday giving. I reassure her that I really like her idea about sharing an experience instead of another store-bought gift, and it's true. I love the idea of doing something intergenerational, the three of us ladies together.

The Vienna Boys Choir is playing on CBC radio like

some kind of royal hint. Mom's heard about a choir from a trusted friend who gave it a rave review. I've never heard of this trusted friend, but on this recommendation, along with Mom's heightened insistence and my understanding of her musical taste, I find Mom's laptop and search up the webpage of the show.

It's Mom's idea and her present so I want her to feel that we are doing this together. I lift her feet off the sofa so I can sit close and so Mom can watch her daughter perform another genius miracle. The choir is booked at one of the city's few bona fide cathedrals, a detail which seems to cure Mom's headache. We scroll through gorgeous photos of the cathedral and admire its Gothic style. We learn that it was built in 1901 and modelled after the famous Chartres cathedral in France. Mom's spirits have lifted, and mine have too, and we exchange satisfied looks. Mom has taught me so much about art and culture through travel and music. It's been a while since we admired the inside of a church or bought tickets to the symphony. As I study the available seating plan, Mom's vision of angelic sounds, of heavenly sopranos and heartbreaking falsettos in a beautiful setting takes shape in my imagination. I am so filled with antici-pation that it doesn't occur to me to do any extra digging about the performance itself.

Mom grew up in Sweden, and the way she talks about her childhood cultural sensibilities is part nostalgia for the old ways, part fierce pride at having left it all behind. Her upbringing was about opera and polished silverware, lit candles and handwritten notes. She's successfully passed at least the last two on to my siblings and me, things that show an inkling of proper upbringing and classy taste. She frequently slams North America as "having zero cultural finesse" which I always take a bit personally, since Canada is the motherland she chose and loves and birthed us all into. She's not wrong, but it strikes me as an unfair shot against Canada considering the thousand years Europe has on us. I think a lot of European immigrants struggle to appreciate the uniqueness of Canadian culture.

The concert is on December 15, which is six weeks away, and is nearly sold out. I swear, people must book these things while they're still sucking on their kids' Halloween candy. I find the last three adjacent seats and confirm the order. "Done! Mom, this is a wonderful idea. This is going to be perfect. It's a wonderful present." Mom puts her old arms around me in a trembly little hug. "I just want to get into the Christmas spirit. I want you and my granddaughter to hear something I know is very beautiful for Christmas."

When I get home, my teenage daughter's reaction to her grandmother's gift involves such dramatic eye-rolling that I threaten to rush her to emergency to fix her problem. I'm going to have to coax up some strong, magical powers to make Mom's gift enjoyable for her too.

Sure enough, even though my girl is mature enough to have digested and accepted her grandmother's wishes, she's not about to make it easy for me. When December 15 comes around, I have to strong-arm my sweet teen to dress nicely for the concert. Bullying is my last resort since now we're in a rush and I'm hard-pressed to find any kind of deal-sweetener between *church* and *concert*.

We are four minutes late to Mom's and she's waiting outside like she's missed a bus. A light snow is blowing around and her long black coat and matching beret are polka-dotted white. She shivers like she's been standing there abandoned for an hour and hoists herself into the front seat without shaking the snow off her shoulders, which makes me think that she thinks I should have done that for her. Mom shuts the door a little bit hard and doesn't say much as we wait for my daughter to put Mom's rolling walker in the trunk. I whisper to my girl to get Mom's cane as well, just in case. I don't know what kind of headache Mom's got today but I decide not to lean into it. Instead, I conjure Monty Python's "Always Look on the Bright Side of Life" in my head and turn into my best, positive daughter and mother self.

I know I'm not fooling anyone with the inane chitter-chatter that keeps chirping out of my mouth, but it's what I do when Mom starts slipping down that rabbit hole. I could have thought to let some nice soothing music on the radio do its calming work instead. Sandwiched between Mom's emotional fragility and my daughter's surliness, it's a good thing I'm not prone to either.

December 15 is the tried and true, absolute worst kind of Saturday for trying to get anywhere. Planning an outing on December 15 is like signing up for a day of driving at a snail's pace on high, white-knuckled alert. People will do the rudest things as they beeline to the next shopping mall, one eye on their kids' wish list and the other on the clock. If Mom was driving, we would have been all crashed up by now. Not because she's trying to get her Christmas shopping done, because she's not doing any this year, but because traffic makes her even more scattered and jumpy than the www.

Traffic makes me jittery too, and I don't want to add to whatever Mom's fretting about today but I'll be damned if that Lexus will jump his turn to merge, no way, I'm holding firm on my position, Buddy Boy. The stress I'm hiding in my sing-songy voice gathers up in my neck, and my shoulders are pushing into my ears, and we're not even on the bridge yet. I decide right then that all I want for Christmas this year is a deep-tissue massage.

We hack our way through town unscathed and Mom has relaxed a little since I've pulled the trick of passing her the talking stick. She can really be like a water faucet, and once that valve has opened, it's like a direct line to Niagara Falls or the Cleveland Dam. She's launched into her earliest memories of Christmas in Sweden, about the special pickled herring my *morfar* used to make, and how when she was twelve, she and her older naughty siblings stole mind-altering sips of aqvavit when the kitchen maid wasn't looking. I make a mental note to let her do all the talking more often, seeing as how much calmer she gets when I let her have control. I make another mental note to get myself a kitchen maid and also to stock up on aqvavit.

Mom is mid-tale about dragging some forty-five-foot-tall spruce tree behind the family Volvo as I get to our destination and I idle right in front of the cathedral to let everyone out. I crane my neck over the steering wheel to get a better view of the intricate neo-gothic stone rose window that towers above us. The fine relief of the carving is dusted with snow that gives it a highlighted 3D effect. Just like the photos, this cathedral is mightily impressive with its two uneven towers, a sight which should please Mom, but she's back to fiddling with her purse. All cheery and oozing with patience, I wait until she's found her lipstick, then gently nudge her to gather herself up. Mom's been on the knee replacement surgery wait list for so long it's starting to feel like a sort of cruel punishment. To convenience my passengers, I've inconvenienced some prize champ in the lane behind me who starts blaring his horn. He stops only when my daughter produces Mom's walker and cane from the trunk and I think how my darling had better be giving him some of that killer eye-rolling she's been perfecting on me. Mom calls her walker "Johnny Walker" and I wonder why I don't laugh at more of her jokes. Mom has always rebelled against social conventions, and since the dastardly plague of oldness has taken hold, her jokes have taken on a darker edge. She even calls her handicapped parking tag her "gimp pass." I think her jokes sometimes hit a little close to my own fears of getting old.

Even with the help of my daughter, who's unfolded Johnny Walker and holds out her hand to help Mom out of the car, Mom takes her sweet time steadying her footing on the snowy pavement. I give her a solid point for acting like she's half paralyzed for the prolonged benefit of Mr. Hot Holy Honks whose face goes from impudent to humble in my rear-view mirror.

If driving was a nightmare, then parking is hell. I circle around the block in some kind of existential test of patience. By the time I find a parkade not already jammed with righteous shoppers, I'm feeling pretty hot under the arms. The snowflakes are coming down fat and fluffy as I hurry back to the front of the venue. I spot Mom on the steps of the cathedral, right at the front of the long line that snakes around the entire block and out of sight. She's making a big deal about Johnny Walker, clattering it around, and my daughter lifts it over the top step as I stride up to join them.

"Gimps shouldn't have to wait this long," says Mom to

the frozen couple she's cut in front of, never mind they'd probably been waiting there for two years already. She might hate needing Johnny, but she's sure not shy about wielding him around like a solid gold VIP pass.

We find our spots in the middle of the long, wooden pew. My responsibility as driver and coordinator shifts to warden and officer of comfort and I sit between my charges so as to monitor their Christmas spirit equally. I should have clued into the guaranteed uncomfortable sitting arrangement implied by the word 'cathedral,' especially one modelled after a French one from the thirteenth century. There's probably some thousand-year-old papal decree about discomfort as proof of godliness or maybe it's just the oldest trick in the book to keep people from getting too cozy and falling asleep during Mass. Either way, I should have thought to bring a pillow for Mom. Whenever she comes for dinner, she orders the grandchildren to fetch her a pillow, and sometimes she even wants two. The look on Mom's face says I should have remembered too, so I take off my coat and fold it into a square so she can sit on it like a cushion. Today, Mom is the one who is supposed to be in control—it's her concert, her present. I try to make a joke about how much she'll enjoy her new booster seat.

It feels old and grand in the sanctuary, if anything in post-colonial Canada can be considered old, with ornate details on every surface of the interior. Which is excellent for keeping both teenager and grandmother occupied in active-detail-observation mode. I point out three lovely oak altarpieces that are backed by a carved screen and covered in gold foliage.

Mom tells us the screen is called a reredos and explains that it comes from the Latin word *dorsum*, meaning rear. I'm always impressed when she pulls out random factoids like this, how she really perks up at any old classical segues, plucking from her deep reserve of old languages and the old European ways. Mom keeps rearranging and slipping around on my coat and I hope I didn't leave my glasses in the pocket. I shift attention to the massive organ beside the main altar. Mom knows a thing or two about pipe organs despite never having been a churchgoer.

One summer when my brother and I were teenagers, Mom took us on a European tour through Sweden, Germany, and France. Over five weeks, I learned to drive stick on the Autobahn, raced through Grand Est to speed as fast as the French, side-swiping my way through cobble-stoned Parisian traffic, all to arrive at Eglise Saint-Sulpice, Mom's idea of Mecca. As soon as she'd finished thanking God for sparing us in a fiery wreck, Mom resumed her secular philosophy: cathedrals were places of utmost sacred beauty, just as long as there wasn't too much of God in the picture. And that you didn't need to love God to love churches. Even after weeks of dragging two know-it-all, back-talking high-schoolers into places we never would choose to go, Mom's determination to show us majesty in architecture and sound never faltered. If it was up to my brother and me, we would have ignored all those soaring arches and Corinthian capitals, our eyes and ears pushed down into our immature selves. But Mom knew better. She said, "Listen!"

Which was all it took for us to pay attention, to stop thinking about our self-importance for ten seconds, a tiny pause that turned into a trick of two minutes and then twelve and then almost a whole hour of letting the mind-blowing sound of seven thousand organ pipes reverberate into every cell of our bodies. For Mom, God was in beauty and music. She entrusted cathedrals to do the teaching for her, knowing that just being in these exquisite spaces would be enough to imprint something of her passions onto our inexperienced senses.

Mom has found enough purchase on my coat to consider the organ *du jour*. She thinks this one has something like twenty-five hundred pipes and I hope that they will be enough.

People are still filing in and we have to stand up a silly amount of times to let them shuffle past us along the pew. Coat-cushion management has turned into a full-time job. People-watching has become my teenager's point of interest. She starts whispering and giggling at some of the mismatched get-ups around us and I shush her with a motherly scolding look combined with a conspiring smile. Mom's doing the same thing on my other side, only instead of finding things funny, she's pointing out her disdain for jeans and sneakers in the crowd. Mom despises snobs, so when she's the one acting snobby, I reason what she's really saying is that she just wants all these people to respect the special occasion of being entertained here in one of the city's few bona fide cathedrals. Casual attire seems flippant in a place where Mom expects respect and I have to agree. She seems to take the sloppy efforts around us as personal insults. I just pray that Mom won't turn her head enough to notice a couple of middle-aged men sitting directly behind us wearing ball caps. For Mom, wearing a ball cap, inside, is a criminal act, offensive enough to support her entire zero-cultural-finesse theory and then some.

The choir pours out from doors that flank the reredos on either side of the sanctuary. The singers attempt to glide soft-footed in single file around the entire perimeter of the room. If an impression of stealth is the overall idea, they're going at it more like clowns than ninjas. It's a men's choir, and about half of them are wearing dorky felted reindeer headbands like the kind I bought at the dollar store for my kids when they were about four years old.

The crowd goes silent while the grinning performers align themselves shoulder to shoulder. Every second singer is holding a wooden rod with rows of bells attached. There's a stock-still pause that lets everyone know that something major is about to happen. And boy, does it ever.

Four more men burst forth from the back doors in twosomes, blasting out like horses through a starting gate to meet up in the middle aisle. A couple of long, wooden sticks are produced and held in horizontal positions along both sides of the foursome to make a sort of pantomimed Santa sleigh. Then someone lets out a terrific whistle, the type some people can make with a couple of fingers in their mouth, like they're calling a dog out of a ditch. But it's not a dog, it's yet another prancing man, this one bearded and heavy-set, decked out in a full reindeer costume with the baggy brown suit and a big red nose and antlers and, oh wow, he's leaping up to the front of the so-called sleigh to complete the ensemble, with his full-grown man hooves bent up coyly under his chin. And this is the signal to every North American to burst into applause, which everyone around us does with gusto.

My teenager laughs, but not in a joyful Christmas spirit laugh, something more maniacal, a my-stomach-muscles-will-be-sore-in-the-morning kind of laugh. She can hardly clap, she's laughing so hard. I think her reaction is exaggerated but not entirely inappropriate. I'm just relieved she's found some version of fun.

On the other side of me, Mom isn't clapping.

Her posture is crumpled, and her worrying hands are busy picking off her beautiful manicure, which isn't an easy thing to do if you've ever had that kind of car paint cured onto your nails. There's a pile of ruby-red flakes on the flagstone by her feet.

Someone starts hitting those snappy yuletide sticks together and the singers are on the move. They trot into standard choir formation at the front of the sanctuary to launch into their first song, which any idiot, including Rudolph, could guess was going to be "Jingle Bells." I mean, they could hardly make such a big deal about all those bells and the clever sleigh contraption and then leave us all hanging.

The men's voices come together in a rich, resonating a cappella; their sound is something strong and splendid. That is, if you like North American Christmas carols. The killing bit is when the director of the choir starts running into the pews, singling people out and encouraging everyone to sing along. I mean, I like to sing, but singing on demand with a group of ragtag strangers like this is embarrassing, and besides, I only know the words of Christmas carols up until about the first verse. And they're really going for it, the full nine yards of every song, including all the B-side verses. It's not like I've never heard carols, of course. It's not that I haven't sung them either. It's just that I've never felt an urgency for them to be over and done with for the sake of someone else's sanity. By the look on Mom's face, she had no idea that "Jingle Bells" had four verses either.

I sense Mom's deep cringe plummet as we're led down the merrily-told, epic saga of Miss Fanny Bright and her beloved horse who gets them all drifted into some snow bank. The nerdy part of me is glad to know the full extent of this perennial favourite but mostly it's a painful time of pretending to know the words and clapping along to avoid looking like some Scrooge.

My daughter has found a certain unbridled joy in the terribleness. There are tears running down her face, she's so beyond. One side of my body is laughing with her, wanting to be her partner in parody, and the other side is holding Mom's hand, partly to keep her spirits buoyant, partly to make sure she doesn't feel alone, and partly to stop further destruction of her manicure.

Mom looks like she might have tears too. This is not her music, not her vibe, not her taste. Not her expectation, which was probably more along the lines of "Ave Verum Corpus" but Mozart was never even invited to this party. It occurs to me that Mom might not actually know any of the words to any of these songs. It's no wonder she's fidgeting like crazy. She's looking past the choir at the organ that is gathering dust and spittle at best. Those twenty-five hundred pipes would be in full swing if we were watching the Vienna Boys Choir like Mom wanted instead of this a cappella show.

Beyond not holding the door and forgetting a pillow, the weight of my greatest oversight presses down on me. If only I were half the genius Mom thinks I am, I'd have spent an extra minute or two on the www before rushing to buy the tickets. I could have made sure that Mom knew what to expect today. If only I had slowed down, I might have averted what she is making look like a real tragedy. I wonder if Mom still thinks I'm a genius, or if she's rethinking her friendship with the person who recommended this in the first place. I wonder if she just feels like everything's her fault.

My coat is trailing on the floor. The choir works their way through the expected roster of yuletide hits and I belt out as many as I can, because the only thing I can do right now is to go with this flow. Besides, I'm ready to surrender to the version of Christmas spirit that surrounds us. I want Mom to feel it too but I can't seem to infect her with the lighter side of things, not even with my most earnest pretend-singing of the gruelling dead march of "Good King Wenceslas," which has the nerve to contain five verses. I only know about half of the first line of that dirge. The choir is so good, they make it sound pretty upbeat. My daughter wipes tears of hilarity with the sleeve of her coat at my toneless drone. I swear, this is the most she's ever cried since she was a tiny little baby. I can hardly believe she has any tears left.

The whole thing ends with an emphatic, "We Wish You a

Merry Christmas," and I accept with gratitude. Sometimes, when you pretend to enjoy something, you end up actually enjoying it. Even my daughter knows the words to this one, and she's actually singing along. I wish so hard for some merriment to permeate Mom. This song, out of all of them, is not about cradles and messiahs and old-timey anachronisms. It's about the gift of spirit that Mom longs for and is something that everyone wants, no matter if they're getting a load of presents this year or not. It's the epitome of North American culture to be so pointedly unpoetic, to compose a song that literally tells you: Here is the Christmas spirit, it's for you and your whole family, take it, take some more, here you go, you're welcome!

The whole place is wall-to-wall with shiny, happy faces. Joyful. Jubilant, even in ball caps. There's no denying the Christmas spirit that fills this elaborate space, looking us all right in the face, in plain English. Maybe it's the English that's the problem. Maybe Mom just wanted to hear it in Latin.

Her mobility was pretty good on our way in but now, as we shuffle our way between pews to join the slow plod towards the exit, Mom's knees straight-up no longer work. She stumbles, shuffles, cries out in pain. Johnny Walker is not enough and she doesn't want her cane. She reaches for my daughter and me for stability. She hurts me a little, pinching into my arm and pulling on my sleeve in rough tugs. It's as though she wants me to feel something of the longing that is piercing her heart. I imagine that her disappointment has shifted like a physical thing into her bones and the weight of it is enough to buckle her knees. Her dashed expectations show up in the frailness of her body, which refuses to participate. Maybe she's caught between the demons of her psyche, arcing from past regrets to future anxieties. I think that sometimes her chronic pain is the only thing that brings her back into the present. "This headache," she says, right on cue.

Someone thoughtful has swept the light covering of snow off the sidewalk and the skies have lifted. I put the brakes on Johnny and turn Mom's shoulders towards me so I can gather her up in a big bear hug. The three of us will never visit Vienna but we are Here, three generations together, and Here has to be enough.

I didn't see that cliché coming about presence being the real present but here it is, and it's not even cheeseball this time because it's so true.

Mom's gotten so short and small, she feels almost childlike in my arms. She smells like Swedish baking, of ginger and fresh green cardamom. It's strange to think how it wasn't so long ago that I held my daughter like this. Mom's breath hitches fast on my neck.

Mom says into my neck, "I don't know how many more chances I have to get things right." My daughter, who has grown into the world's least huggish person, steps closer and wraps her arms around Mom from the back.

"Oh, Mom. There are so many things you got right," and my beautiful daughter smiles at me over Mom's head when I say it. It's been a while since she's given me a real smile like that.

We hold her and hold her and hold her, until we've hugged every one of Mom's seventy-nine Christmases, the wrong ones and the right ones and all the ones in the middle.

Until she hugs us back.

The Harlequin Set

JJ LEE

My grandfather sold his share of the Dragon Room restaurant in Chomedey, Quebec, to his uncle and cousins. With the money, Gung-gung settled on a small plot in Saint-Eustache. The farm's property lines revealed its origins in New France. It lay on the north side of the Rivière du Chêne on a former seigneurial tract that once stretched to a screen of trees on the horizon. Sometime after 1752, a *chemin* parallel to the river split the property in two. Gung-gung owned the nine acres between the river and the road. There he and Poh-poh grew Chinese vegetables like bak choi, gai lan, and ong choi.

As a child, I didn't know any of this. I had no idea that they had immigrated in 1964. I assumed my grandparents had always lived here and were part of the land as much as the old barn, the mighty oak in the front, or the pond with its unknown depth. I thought the farm was an eternal fact of my life.

My memories of the place can be reduced to two seasons: summer and Christmas.

Summer was all about kite-flying (my grandfather could

make them out of scraps of bamboo and garbage bags), taking the green boat out on the river to fish (without a life jacket), and handling shotguns, rifles, and Czechoslovakian air rifles without adult supervision (which would have landed those adults in jail today).

Christmas involved driving to the farm from Saint-Lambert on Christmas Day, the Oldsmobile ploughing through an ocean of snow like some great landship, and arriving to find the old farmhouse filled with uncles, aunts, cousins, friends, Poh-poh, Gung-gung, and a tree in the corner. Under its boughs, my extended family would pile fifty or sixty presents, mostly for my brother, my sisters, my cousins, and me. I could tell you about zipping Hot Wheels cars down the orange tracks, or the Danish butter cookies that come in blue tins, or the clack of mah-jong tiles against the table after Christmas dinner, but lately my mind keeps returning to one particular memory that could have been forgotten forever if it hadn't been for my son Jack.

I'm sure I've jumbled up the details, but here goes: I'm eleven. We've come to the farm a day or two before Christmas. I share a room with Uncle Philip, who uses the box spring while I sleep on a mattress on the floor. Philip is only a year and a half older than me, and at times we are more like cousins or brothers, but secretly he's a hero to me. He is taller and more athletic, and, because he skipped a grade, he already plays on a basketball team. Usually my first overnight stay since Thanksgiving would mean a long conversation until late. In the dark, he would give me the latest on high-school life and maybe even girls. Sometimes he focused on something he was puzzling over, but I was always too young to be of any help.

This time our conversation veers to why our family celebrates Christmas. Why we aren't religious. Why we don't believe in Christ. Maybe we do it for the children. Or to bring the family together. Or because it's fun. Neither Philip nor I consider that we do it because we want to fit in, to make a claim to this place, to belong. Our late-night ramble goes from topic to topic, and somewhere between does-God-exist and who-is-the-perfect-girl or some such, we drift off to sleep.

The next morning I wake up earlier than everyone else. The floor is cold. The vast kitchen is flooded with an even grey light. There's a humongous laundry machine on the right. Beside it is the freezer, big enough to stuff a moose inside. On the left, a long counter stretches past the sink to a refrigerator stuffed with provisions for Christmas dinner. In the centre of the room is a dining table that seats six, but they'll add two more, making enough space for sixteen. With maximum attendance, there will be four of Gung-gung and Poh-poh's children, four children's spouses or dates, eight grandchildren, and three or four friends—about twenty-two people around the tables here and a set of the youngest children in the living room eating over the coffee table.

Soon a mountain of food will cover all of them: winter melon soup, dumplings, rice rolls, baked lobster, roast beef, crackling pork, turkey, tourtière, war su gai, Chinese boneless chicken. Perhaps this is an image of all my Christmases put together, or maybe that's exactly how the table will be laden. But now I'm alone and I just want a bowl of cereal and a glass of orange juice.

The cupboard to the right of the sink holds small A&W root beer steins, curvy Coca-Cola glasses, white CorningWare mugs, and tumblers printed with hearts, diamonds, spades, and clubs. I think the last were originally mustard jars. In the cupboard to the left of the sink, the plates and bowls are decorated with waterfalls, phoenixes, pagodas, and dragons. They must have come from the Dragon Room. For some reason, I notice how the pattern is worn. The images are faded, ground away by customers' forks and knives in a way chopsticks never could. I also notice how thick and tough they are. Indeed, they have been handled roughly, probably for years, tossed in and out of commercial dishwashers who knows how many times before coming here. On some plates, the glaze has worn through to expose the near-unbreakable, industrial-grade ceramic underneath. They remind me of my grandfather's back: broad, rounded, and hard like a granite boulder.

It is only a passing moment of recognition. I take one of those bowls, eat my cereal, and have my Christmas. I grow up, move to Vancouver, marry, raise my own family, and forget about that quiet morning at Gung-gung's farm.

My grandfather died in 2012. The property had to be sold. My mother and sisters considered buying it as well as the land across the road to reunite and restore the seigneurial plot. Eventually my mother nixed the idea. Her words came from a well of hurt to which I had no access. She decreed, "The past is the past. Let it die."

I already had, I suppose. By the time they sold the farm, all my childhood Christmases had become shimmers and glows, shadows and veils of dawn. Always yearned for but nothing of substance to hold on to. I did my best to create the same magic with my own children—but what I had felt as a child, I could no longer access.

Then one evening, six months after Gung-gung passed, it all came back to me. My son Jack, who was nine, stared down at his cleared dinner plate and said, "It's depressing."

He meant the pattern on the only matched set of dishware my wife Melissa and I owned. The blue-on-white design is called Riverwood. Melissa and I both knew the theme was autumnal, but we had no clue what Jack was talking about.

The set came from the basement of the Hudson's Bay on Granville Street. The budget-housewares department was actually a sub-basement below menswear and shouldn't be confused with the fifth floor, with the fine china and crystal. Before marrying Melissa, I thought of the sub-basement as an alternative route to get from the street to the SkyTrain platform. It was the place where people bought knock-off Bodum, plastic-handled knives, and kitchen gizmos as seen on TV. In truth, back then, I really couldn't say what they sold. I was a lousy homemaker.

The day Melissa moved in with me, she discovered just how lousy. I owned a fork, a spoon, a table knife, two rice bowls, two pairs of chopsticks, a pot big enough to make a single serving of instant ramen, and a small cast-iron pan I'd found in a dollar store. My wife, however, insists there was no fork.

The first meal I made for her we ate off the top of a box covered in a Mexican blanket. That dinner should have been reason enough for Melissa to abandon a life with me, but she didn't.

We got married a month later. She was in Canada on a travel visa, and getting hitched was the only way she could stay. No one from Melissa's family came from Australia for the civil ceremony. There wasn't time. Nanna Stephens, though, sent money as a wedding gift. When the cheque arrived in the mail, Melissa said, "She made me promise we'd use it to buy some dishes."

The Riverwood came with four settings made up of a dinner plate, side plate, bowl, and cup and saucer. Instinctively, I liked the blue-and-white pattern.

I picked up Jack's plate to have a closer look. A flock of geese against a dreary sky, flying south to escape the cold. I went to the cupboard and checked the other Riverwood pieces. For the first time, I really studied them. Each was decorated with a rural vignette: a fallen fence, bare-branch trees, collapsing barn, or a hay wagon with a broken wheel. Jack was right. The dishes were bleak as hell. Only now, in retrospect, I realize that the pattern was my bridge back to the crowded meals around Gung-gun and Poh-poh's table. With those dishes, I'd tried in my own life to evoke moments from the farm.

The Riverwood has served as the backdrop for auspicious moments. I'm not the type to photograph food, and nor is Melissa, but I do have one nice picture from a beautiful summer day when I made *faisan à la vigneronne* with grapes, cognac, and *crème fraîche* to celebrate my forty-fifth birthday. Okay, I used chicken instead of pheasant, but the sense of *plaisance* was as real and as Gallic as it gets. The blue-and-white pattern can hardly be seen, yet it is there—part of the story.

The Riverwood has never seen the inside of a dishwasher. Our first place was a basement suite on Burnaby Street in Vancouver, and dishwashers were not allowed. The sink sat in a dark corner, which may explain why I never noticed the pattern. Our second apartment, on Queens Avenue in New Westminster, had the same restriction against dishwashers, but the kitchen sink was amazing. While washing and rinsing by hand, you could look out the window and, from time to time, witness the corner drug deals. I mostly watched the wind sway the branches of the nearby birch.

We couldn't stay there forever. The apartment was fine when it was just Melissa and me, but then we had Jack and his twin, Emmet, making it four people with just one bedroom. We had our queen-sized bed and two cribs jammed in there. I hate to admit it, but the boys used those cribs until they were eight. There just wasn't enough floor space.

By the time we moved out of Queens Avenue, we had lost most of our Riverwood. The day we packed to move to a two-bedroom on Seventh, I counted four bowls but only three big dishes. Just one side plate remained.

As for the cups and saucers, they had all been snapped, dropped, or shattered. I finished off the last cup while

✳

washing it. I pushed a sponge a bit too hard into the cup, then I heard a snap and felt a tremor through my fingertip. The cup clattered on top of the dishes in the sink. The handle remained between my thumb and index finger.

Since Jack's observation, we haven't bothered replacing lost Riverwoods. Instead, Melissa decided on English ceramics with white or cream bases, gold edging, and floral or fruit patterns. The older the better. They didn't need to match. Montreal Crockery's King Edward pattern alongside Crown Ducal Florentine, Hammersley's Peony, Johnson Brothers Posy, Royal Albert Holly, were all found one piece at a time at thrift shops—which is where, I assume, the dishes from Gung-gung and Poh-poh's ended up.

According to a friend who is very British and knows these things, a collection of mismatched dishes is called a harlequin set. When I heard that, I felt relieved. Until then, the hodgepodge nature of our dishware—and, really, our life in general—was starting to get me down. At times, it feels as if we haven't moved beyond our days of eating off the top of a box. Sometimes naming a condition, a circumstance, or a state of life (or dishware, in this case) confers dignity. It was just what I needed to hear. I became proud of our harlequin set.

My family has its own Christmas traditions now. In the morning, we invite friends and neighbours to our suite for a yuletide breakfast. I use two leaves to extend the oak gateleg table. Melissa fries mushrooms and boils a dozen eggs. I bake rashers of bacon and warm a pile of Portuguese buns. Melissa puts on tea and coffee. I lay out a board of cheese. Alongside all this, on a white tablecloth, we add Melissa's mince tarts, two small jars of cheap caviar, and Quality Street chocolates that sparkle in their gem-coloured wrappers. And, finally, we set the table with our strange collection of mismatched white and cream dishes, our harlequin set.

Christmas isn't like my childhood. There is no farm. And seven people isn't quite twenty-two. Still, the dining room fills with talk and laughter and the scrape and clink of dishes and glasses. My mother was wrong. The past isn't the past. Some things never die.

Forty Dollarama Cards

JORDAN KAWCHUK

The sober house was a two-storey Vancouver Special deep in a rough part of Surrey. Sober homes don't function in nice neighbourhoods, leading to the cruel irony that those either wanting or ordered to be sober are mere steps away from drugs, liquor stores, and never coming back.

The men who got caught relapsing or sneaking in substances were immediately booted out. Their belongings hurriedly thrown into black garbage bags, not-so-lovingly known in sober house circles as Surrey Suitcases.

Temptation was the main reason we were not permitted out of the house for the first week. In Weeks 2 and 3, we were permitted to sign out and walk in groups of three. Finally, after one month, we would get solo privileges.

I had come to Fleetwood Manor (a name that gave me endless joy, as there was nothing manor-like about it) following two months in a professional treatment centre for Alcohol Use Disorder—the gentler, more modern term doctors and therapists use today for being an alcoholic.

It's often recommended to live in a sober house or "second stage" after a stint in treatment to avoid a jarring transition from the safe bubble of rehab to immediate home life.

I, of course, wanted to come straight home and continue life with my new tools and an inspired outlook. My partner, Lauren, wasn't ready for me to come home. She had been burned too many times. I had a little slip back in treatment and they forgave, but it didn't win me very much with the ones who mattered most on the outside.

Also, this wasn't my first time in treatment. This wasn't my first sober house stay.

The world narrows dramatically inside a sober house so that the smallest events or changes in routine can turn epic. And for us in Fleetwood Manor, after Week 1, the five-block walk to the Dollarama was the most important part of our day. A trip to the Dollarama meant freedom. It was the independence of buying little things. Junk food to hoard, candy to barter with, and if no one stole it from the fridge, it meant a root beer or cream soda to look forward to.

The Dollarama was Disneyland.

Tip: if you ever want to know where a Dollarama is located, just follow the slow trail of men in hoodies, high-tops, and sweatpants, chain-smoking. They'll eventually lead you to the green and yellow sign on the next corner.

When I was still on mid-restrictions, I was required to find at least two other guys to go with. I joined Nate, a newer addition to the house who had a tattooed neck and rarely spoke, and Calvin, a gym rat with a cast on his left arm. There was also Eric, a guy closer to my age who collected music biographies and had the same pop culture tastes as me, and Baseball Manny. We wrote our names and the time in a book that sat upon a podium in the front hallway and walked out into the frosty December outside world.

Cigarettes and vape pens were immediately ignited, like cowboy quickdraws. We took our time. Not only were we in no rush to get back, no one at this stage in sobriety was very interested in fast walking. Our bodies needed chips and pop, not exercise.

"I'm gonna fuckin' kill Bruce," said Calvin. "Says I can't stay overnight at my baby mama's place for Christmas."

"Pretty sure no one gets overnights, bro," said Eric. "You know that."

"Fuck him anyway."

We passed a house with its front lawn overgrown with inflatable Santas, Rudolphs, and off-brand characters I couldn't name. A couple were half-deflated and looked like they had suffered strokes.

"Anyone got ten bucks they can spot me?" Calvin asked, changing the topic.

"You're already into me for forty," said Baseball Manny.

"Last time, I swear."

A walk like this, with Christmas signifiers, just as it began to lightly snow, made me a bit sick with displacement and a yearning for home.

Lauren and I would talk over the phone every night—her from our home in Vancouver, me from the porch of Fleetwood Manor, before the 10:00pm curfew when we surrendered our cell phones to the house manager. There was never much privacy, so I always found myself speaking low into the microphone on my headphones, like I was a secret service agent.

Lauren and I had loving conversations that pointed toward progress, but there was always an underlying, unspoken current of uncertainty. Me waiting to be asked home. Her, careful not to bruise me with tales from a normal world.

"A few of us went out after work, nothing exciting. The usual, teacher talk, nachos."

"We had leftover spaghetti tonight. But someone keeps stealing giant scoops out of my ice cream."

"Don't you write your name on your stuff?"

"Hun, I live with a bunch of addicts."

And I did. Most of them referred to themselves as addicts. They were fighting addictions to (and combinations of) cocaine, meth, crack, fentanyl, opioids, and heroin. Whereas I called, and still call, myself an alcoholic.

Over the two decades of managing and mismanaging

my condition and needing to reboot myself in treatment, I'm always a rarity wherever I go. In fact, I've been called a 'dying breed' even though alcohol is widely known as the hardest one to kick and the only addiction withdrawal you can die from. Still, it's seen as milquetoast and old school. Like I should be riding the rails in a crumpled fedora, holding a bottle of moonshine labelled XXX.

"You mean you're just an alcoholic?"

"Yup," I say.

"Dude. You're like, so old."

Only Eric and I entered the Dollarama. The rest hung back for one more smoke. The lighting was brighter than a doctor's examination room. The floors were spackled grey like hospital halls. I looked at the seemingly endless aisles barfing cheap goods. All of it I suddenly felt I needed to *own*.

The summer gardening aisles were filled with holiday stuff. Fuzzy Santa and striped elf hats drooped next to sparkly snowflakes to hang, cheap plastic wreaths, rubber nativity animals, and tree ornaments already peeling their paint. There were miles of candy canes.

The tinsel and artificial trees jogged a memory. I never really grew up with real fragrant firs for Christmas trees. My brother had allergies. I settled into the idea that the store's fakeness felt both unsettling and familiar.

The guys, including me, loaded their baskets with Doritos, dozens of energy drinks (a sober house food group), spare lighters, marshmallow cereal, handfuls of peanut butter cups, bags of sour worms, expired Halloween value packs, and piles of neon licorice. But I also saw boxes of holiday cards on my way to the cashier.

A sudden urge to reach out, to reconnect, and dust off my heart burned in me. What if I sent Christmas cards to people I may have hurt or who had since forgotten about me? I mean, it's not the official 12-Step amendment process I would eventually have to face, but it was sort of goodwill, right? I wouldn't even have to mention my last few months, which had been mired in relapse, shame, rehab, finance, and relationship crashes . . . I didn't even have to mention I was living in a rehab, right?

I grabbed four boxes of ten and paid for my stuff. We walked back, even slower than the journey up, mostly in silence as we all cracked open our chips and tasted freedom from a bag. The cards sat on my thrift store dresser in the room I shared with Manny for a few days. I didn't know where to start. They were all cheap drugstore-quality greeting card stock printed identically with a corny cartoon cover of penguins playing in the snow.

Eventually, I scrolled through forgotten friends and old colleagues on social media and made the most ragtag out-of-the-blue list. I cut and pasted the same request for their mailing addresses into messages for seventy-five unsuspecting people. Sure, the list included close family and friends, but the majority were people I hadn't spoken to in years. Some responded with enthusiastic catch-up paragraphs, some simply pinged their particulars, and a lot asked, "Why?" or "What the fuck?" Some never responded at all.

I hadn't sent a card to anyone for over two decades. Most likely when I was married a lifetime ago, and it was common for young couples with a new baby to invest in glossy and merry family photo cards, a rambling letter recapping the year's highlights neatly folded inside.

Every day, sitting on the worn vinyl couch in the common living room, I chipped away at three or four cards, surrounded by guys watching TV shows—usually *Forged in Fire*, a weapon-making competition series, or one of the many DVDs on hand like *Fast & Furious*.

The messages were simple but the motive was tangled. They were veiled atonements. Unofficial amends. Notes delivered by imaginary carrier pigeons from the front lines, to signal to everyone I was okay.

Merry Christmas, Allison! Loving your family Hawaii pics online! Just wanted to wish you a happy holiday and hope to see you soon!

It's not like I was going to tell anyone about Fleetwood Manor: that there were twelve guys in here at all times; that we slept two to a small bedroom and couldn't choose our roommate, all of us sharing one bathroom; the kitchen being roomy and the common area being used for a lot of hanging around and the occasional 'house meeting' where real tempers came out about who's not making coffee or who snores; or that there was a small office sitting near the front entrance, where a small staff of dudes rotated shifts to do intakes, dole out meds, and take needed breaks from the craziness of early sobriety and testosterone. I wasn't going to tell anyone that the garage was carpeted and decked out with mismatched chairs for our mandatory daily recovery meetings. Some guys took it seriously and shared about their day and their feelings, but some guys fidgeted and grunted through the readings; most just wanted it over so they could smoke or vape outside as soon as possible, the lidless coffee canister outside the back door filling up with butts as quickly as rain.

> *Hey Brad! Hope you're well! I sure miss making*
> *television with you. Are you still doing camera*
> *for the travel show? Merry Christmas, man!*

I should mention that, though I inherently understand the beneficial cushion and routine a sober house can provide after treatment, a sober house is a world away from a treatment centre.

Here's the difference. A good treatment centre is a tightly structured and safe place to heal with group therapy, counselling, lectures, optional yoga and meditation, deep assignments, and nutritious meals. Most people inside are genuinely there to get better, and those who are forced in by hurting families or concerned workplaces eventually feel the shift and work hard to change. Often that shift is spiritual in nature, and even though the average success rate of treatment sticking is something like twenty percent, if you do the work every day during and after treatment, you can eventually rewire your brain, heal your body, and feel love, empathy, selflessness, and self-esteem again for a new way of living.

A sober house, in contrast, is more of a place to crash. Somewhat safe on paper, as you're theoretically living in a substance-free environment, but it's not treatment. You are accountable for chores, your sign-ins and sign-outs, and meetings. But for the most part, it's usually made up of a rougher bunch, some even straight out of prison, all sitting around with not a lot to do.

There are life-changing transformative treatment centres and money-making shithole treatment centres. I've experienced both. But the main problem I have had with the suggestion for me to stay in a sober house after treatment

*

is that it's almost more of a culture shock than returning to regular life. It's incredibly discouraging to go from a place of connectedness, heart-shifting learning, and spiritual inspiration to a bunch of bros talking about cars and pussy.

Sex is always on the mind in a sober house. Force a dozen (mostly young) men to live on top of each other, and watch the conversations turn from universal truths in treatment to non-stop dick jokes. I've never heard more talk about masturbation, balls, or rubbing-one-out than I have in a sober house. Flip-flops are a must in the one shared shower.

It's a very deflating and unhealing atmosphere that begins to erode the inner light I nurtured in treatment. More and more, day by day, that glow flickers and fades in a sober house. It doesn't make me want to drink, but it removes me from the guy I am aspiring to return to.

One of the core principles of sobriety is honesty, but the other day I found myself unintentionally lying to Lauren on our nightly call.

"Today was wonderful, hun," I said. "Our house meeting was fantastic and I'm learning some really great stuff about giving it all away, and surrendering."

"Awww, so happy to hear that, that's so great," she said.

"You guys got the tree up yet?"

"How are the decorations at the Manor?"

"Oh, they're looking pretty good."

They didn't. And I didn't care. In truth, my days were made up of me hiding my nose in my books, someone calling me a fag for reading so much, one guy getting kicked out for using in his room, and a dinner of frozen pizza for the third night in a row. In truth, I just wanted to fucking go home.

Still, I did bond with most of the guys and that made the days bearable.

There was Manny, my roommate, an older Jewish man with a long beard who shared my love of deli and diner history and taught me the insider stats and deep meaning of baseball. I watched every Blue Jays game with him and started to look forward to them.

There was a guy known simply as The German, so obsessed with weightlifting and working out, that I tried to show interest in his own body-focus to stave off any teasing about my growing gut (commonly called 'treatment tummy' due the exorbitant levels of carbs they feed you). I adopted the gym term 'sick gains' and I would tell him I made some sick gains in my library book.

Then there was Bruce, a former chef for celebrities who had come to Vancouver to shoot movies for a month. Once in a while, after what's called Welfare Wednesday, he would buy some creative provisions and doll up our dinners.

There was a quiet First Nations man named Leo who

took me out to his favourite fried chicken joint. Every morning from the porch, he invited me to feed his pet. He'd get me to put nuts on the railing and the same squirrel would always show up. It was a moment of grace and beauty in such an ugly place.

There was a young kid who had a bad case of 'street feet,' a common ailment among those experiencing homelessness, where damp and uncared feet start to rot. The smell was unbearable until Rick, one of the main house staff, threw out his shoes, demanded the kid take a bath, and found him a pair of slippers from the donation bin. Rick had F-U-C-K tattooed across his left four knuckles, and C-O-P-S across his right. Yet, he came across as a favourite grandpa with bizzaro but sage advice on sobriety. He had twenty-one years under his wide belt.

To endear myself to Rick, I asked him what I should get inked on my eight knuckles. Without missing a beat, he said, "Soft skin."

One twenty-something kid named Bailey glommed onto me early, and both warmed my heart and drove me bananas in equal measure. A manic ball of troubled energy, Bailey would vacuum the carpets every morning before wake-up time to burn off his intensity. The two of us would sit together and go over and over each word of the amends letter he was writing his mother. It was only when I saw his mom visit and tell him to stay away for good that I found out it was his seventh apology letter to her. I'm sure every one was heartfelt too.

He saw me as both a father figure and an alien from a different age. I once made the mistake of referring to the remote control as the clicker and the flipper.

"Sorry, I don't speak Old Man," he told me.

Years later, I'd run into one of these guys around Vancouver. We'd have short and awkward sidewalk chats. I would learn Bailey died of a fentanyl overdose. Baseball Manny attempted suicide by drinking bottles of Lysol on a day pass somewhere. Bruce the chef was last spotted homeless, and no one has seen the street-feet kid again.

When I wasn't writing cards, I looked around for little gifts for Lauren. She would sweetly swing by the Manor every week with a care package that always included ice cream, another couple of books, and my mail (mostly bills and bad news). I always liked to throw her something small back.

I would comb the 'beauty' aisle and pick out a three-pack of metallic rainbow barrettes, add a Butterfinger and a mesh bag of chocolate bells. Total gift price: $3.75 before tax. Which was a problem with Dollarama items. There weren't any price tag stickers. The glaring yellow $1.25 squares were directly printed on every package. You couldn't even scrape it off. It was the official stamp of every sober house gift.

Christmas last year, when I was healthy, on track, and had money that wasn't issued from the government, I had taken Lauren to the ornate and historic Hotel Vancouver for a festive sleepover and a no-holds-barred dinner on a street lined with trees wrapped in tiny white lights. Carolers sang in front of the art gallery across the street and a skyscraper-tall outdoor Christmas tree bathed the whole block in colour.

Slowly over the next few days, I felt I was on a mission to mail the forty cards. I was determined to get them out in time. Having them appear in mailboxes around British Columbia before the big day was important to me. It somehow felt accountable not to be late. More mature. Put together. I wrote card after card, the messages growing longer and clearer the further I went.

> *Thinking of you, Erin. You and your kids are looking great. Wow, how they've grown up. Hope you guys have a wicked holiday.*

> *Merry Christmas Cara! Long time no chat, eh? I've been taking a bit of time off to write. Sorry about that weird year at work. I wasn't in a great place. All good now! Hope we can have coffee sometime soon!*

> *Hey man. Just wanted to apologize for what hap-*

pened. Maybe in the new year we can sit down and talk it through. I just want you to know I think of you often and I sincerely hope you and your family have a wonderful Christmas.

On the first day I was allowed to go outside by myself, I followed a slushy path to a tiny post office counter tucked inside an independent hardware store. I guessed it would be about a ten-minute errand. Maybe a little longer with the icy, unshovelled sidewalks. I was the only one in our group to venture to this dinky, rundown strip mall. The Dollarama was in the opposite direction.

Being on my own felt like some sort of gift. I had to dodge a maze of puddles dotted with cigarette butts and McDonald's litter. My sneakers were soaked. But it was a liberating, profanity-free, and vapeless experience. I was by myself for the first time in forever. With my headphones plugged into a playlist I had dubbed Recovery Inspiration, I walked on a high, a coffee in one hand, forty red envelopes in the other.

The hardware store was less hardware and more mish-mash, like the kind of ma-and-pa shop you'd find in a farming community. The small place was claustrophobic with stuff. Bike tires hung from the ceiling, saws and hammers sat next to crafts and yarn. Kettles and toasters, wrenches and shampoo. Here, if you needed something, they probably had it, but you'd never find it on your own.

I waited at the Canada Post counter at the back for a good five minutes. The woman at the front wrapped up a sale and jogged over. I purchased stamps, and as I started sticking them to the envelopes, I had second thoughts on sending them.

The recipients were so damn random, the motive so cloudy. Most of them would be quickly skimmed over and shoved in the family's wall of Christmas cards. Some would go on fridge doors, held up by real estate magnets. Some would baffle or surprise people. All of them would be recycled by the new year.

On the way, I had said my morning prayers and recovery mantras in my head to stay sober another day and to do the next right thing and selfless acts throughout the day. I wanted booze and addiction out of my life so badly, and really thought I had it this time. But I had felt that before a few times too.

I handed them over anyway, thanked the woman, and walked back to Fleetwood Manor.

That evening, after a dinner of frozen pizzas and garlic bread, I called Lauren. I had been careful on these last calls to keep my entitlement and expectations in check, to relinquish control of situations—another hallmark of recovery and living sober. The slogan 'Let Go And Let God' is right up there with 'One Day At A Time' and 'Progress Not Perfection.'

But we were over the halfway mark of December. I needed some clarity, some answers, a plan.

"Lauren, do you think it's maybe time to come home? I'm feeling really strong. Really spiritual."

"Yeah, I can hear that," she said.

"I can't sell you on my sobriety, I can only show you," I said. "And I gotta be honest, I feel stuck living here. I want to try the 'new me' out in the real world. I want to cook again. I want to cuddle. I want to sit in a real coffee shop, drive my car, pet my cats, hang around our bookstore—" I stopped there. I caught myself making this too much about me. I was overdoing it already.

"Yeah," she said. And after a long pause on both our ends, she said, "Let's give it another week and assess it then, okay?"

I sat on the couch and watched re-runs late into the night because Manny snored like a son-of-a-bitch.

Scrambled Liver

JAKI EISMAN

"What's that smell?"

Boyd and I had survived the Christmas Eve commute—bus-ferry-bus, the anticipated traffic jams and holiday chaos—and were standing outside the bus depot, waiting for our ride.

Boyd sniffed the air like a sommelier. "Sulphur, I think."

Does Campbell River always smell like rotten eggs? I wanted to ask, but I was a guest, an outsider, a party-crasher. I had to mind my manners. "Smells . . . industrious?"

"Sure. Like a big, industrious crap."

"Hey! Don't be mean to Scrambled Liver!"

I'd been delighted by this city nickname from the moment I'd learned of it. And my delight in all things childish, aside from actual, human children, cracked Boyd up.

We were a decent couple when we were both laughing.

Campbell River looked nice enough from our vantage point, but it was hard to go wrong on Vancouver Island: the water, the mountains, the greenery.

Boyd's brother, Matty, pulled up in a blue pickup truck, the same one he'd used to help Boyd and me move into our

Vancouver apartment a few months earlier. We hoisted our backpacks into the truck bed and got in.

"Hey, Matty. Merry Christmas."

Matty was a man of few words and many grunts; I was convinced he hated me. That he and Boyd had emerged from the same womb was a testament to the unpredictability of nature. They were both extremely tall, but while Matty was broad and broody, Boyd was skinny, talkative, kinetic.

"Matteeeeeeeeeeeee!" Boyd wiggled, making the upholstery squeak, and Matty chuckled, shaking his head. In spite of their differences, the brothers were close, and sitting between them in the squishy truck I felt like the net in the middle of a ping-pong table. There to separate all the fun.

Matty rolled down the window, letting in cool air, and lit a cigarette. The radio was set to a classic rock station, and I had to use all my restraint to stop from air drumming along to a Kansas song. Boyd thought classic rock was for yahoos, and Matty? Why tempt fate.

Driving towards their mother's house, I started sweating, in spite of the cold. I was nervous, never having met the rest of Boyd's family—his mom, Randa; his sister and his brother-in-law, Penelope and Pete. And now I was about to spend the next few days in their company.

It was December 24, 2001. I was twenty-five and trying not to let my tsunami-level intimacy issues fuck up my first live-in, long-term relationship. I was also about to celebrate Christmas for the first time.

At first glance, the kindergarten classroom, circa 1981, appeared standard. There were clusters of tiny chairs surrounding tiny tables, the latter topped by mason jars filled with paint-flecked brushes. There were colourful posters decorating the walls—Lose yourself in a book—and a cartoon Winnie-the-Pooh with his hand in the honey pot. But on closer inspection, some 'tells' emerged: an Israeli flag, an embossed rendition of the Ten Commandments, a poster detailing the Hebrew alphabet.

Talmud Torah was a school for Jewish children, and I, a Jewish child, was a student there. Half of the day—the Hebrew half—we called our teacher *Morah* (teacher), and she called us *Yeladim* (children) in return. Bearded rabbis taught us biblical stories, both the greatest hits (Adam and Eve, Noah and the Ark), and some deeper cuts (Samson, he of the Schwarzenegger hair).

All of the people I knew were Jewish, and since my after-school activities took place at the Jewish Community Centre, not exactly a hotbed of diversity, opportunities to branch out didn't arise. Within this Semitic bubble I didn't learn much about the wider world. At Christmastime, I was aware that something was happening—the mall suddenly decorated with tinsel, the parents suddenly encouraging their kids to sit on an old man's lap—but I had no idea what 'it' was.

Hanukkah, technically, is a minor Jewish holiday, mostly hyped up for the sake of the kids and the fact that it coincides with Christmas. At home we didn't do much for Hanukkah aside from light the menorah—one candle for each of the eight nights—and eat latkes, potato pancakes fried in so much oil they had to be stacked on paper towels to stop them dripping.

At school we had a Hanukkah pageant each year, costumes, songs and the like, and I have photographic evidence of that first year, 1981. Morah had assigned each of us one of four costumes: Maccabee (rebel warrior), candle, dreidel (spinning top) or latke.

In the photo, my five-year-old self, having clearly drawn the short straw, is dressed as a latke. The costume—an orb of brown construction paper, replete with oil spatter—is blocking my peripheral view and making it impossible to turn my head. I still manage to be giving the candle squad—those mini glam rockers, with their golden streamers and glitter makeup—some covetous side-eye. It is a menacing look, and, if I did not know better, I'd say that was one latke about three seconds away from grabbing one of the Maccabees' prop swords and losing its shit on the lot of them.

I was buzzing with anxiety by the time we got to Boyd's mom's house, a modest one-story bungalow, even though the only objective for the visit was to relax and have a good time. I couldn't even relax around Boyd yet, and we lived together. Most nights, after Boyd fell asleep—snoring softly in bed beside me—I just stared at the wall for hours, worrying, fretting.

But stepping into Randa's was soothing, like stepping into a year-round Christmas store. The house smelled of gingerbread, oranges and cinnamon, and a glittering pine tree stood in the corner in front of a blazing fire. The scene was so wholesome, so *Little House on the Prairie*, I momentarily forgot myself.

Then it dawned on me that I'd never seen Ma or Pa, or any of the Prairie children for that matter, boozing it up to celebrate. Did 'wholesome' and 'alcohol' cancel each other out? My heart stopped for what felt like a full minute. Knowing I wasn't the sort of person who could hack a family weekend without liquid courage, the Amish-ness of the scene sped from quaint to oppressive.

"Hi, sweetie," Randa embraced Boyd, standing on tippy toes to kiss his cheek. Then she turned to me, open and welcoming. "I'm Randa. So glad you could come! Penelope and Pete will be back any minute. They just popped out to get some wine."

Hallelujah! A Christmas miracle.

Randa was a cross between a fairy godmother and a 1950s sitcom mom. She had short grey hair and glasses, a big smile, and a competent way about her, like she had everything organized and under control. As she showed me around the house, I tried to appear less angst-y than usual by pasting a smile on my face until my cheeks ached. I'm sure it was creepy. Very Mona Lisa-meets-*Psycho*.

In the room set aside for Boyd and me, a large oak bed took up most of the space. The duvet was covered with a beautiful blanket, its textured lines of purples and blues reminding me of the lapping waters we'd just left. I resisted the pull inward by forcing my thoughts into words, being conversational. "Did you knit this yourself, Randa?"

"I did! I'm a big knitter, as you'll probably notice over the weekend. Do you knit?"

Only my eyebrows came to mind, but nature abhors a smart-ass. "Nah. I'm not very crafty."

Randa half-smiled—an aversion to crafting was potentially problematic—but Matty saved the day by lumbering out of one of the bedrooms, parka on. "I'm going out to smoke."

I wasn't a smoker, but I also wasn't a non-smoker. Timing was paramount.

"Oh! Can I bum one?"

Randa and Boyd crinkled noses at each other, but they didn't try to stop us. We were adults, free to suck whatever filth into our lungs we chose. I grabbed my coat and followed Matty through the steamy kitchen, out into the covered carport behind the house. He lit me up, and we smoked mostly in silence, aside from a few requisite weather comments ("It's cold." "Yup." "Think it'll snow?" "Might.")

I was a loner by nature—guessed that Matty and I might have that in common—and even learning to spend time with one other person, Boyd, required ongoing adjustments. I hadn't grown up with siblings, or with much family around; I seemed to be deficient in the human-tribal instinct.

Randa's house bordered on a dense urban forest, and, standing smoking under the awning, I had a sudden urge to bolt. To run into these woods, to find a hollow tree, to never be seen or heard from again. I felt completely ill-equipped to be a human amongst other humans, unsure what to say or not to say, how to move my body, where to put myself. Whether a Jew celebrating Christmas or a misfit-Jew celebrating Hanukkah, my discomfort transcended religious lines. I felt trapped, both by my brain and inside of my skin.

Sigh. All smokers know that the time spent burning

through one's cigarette is just time spent postponing the inevitable. Which in this case was a sit-down, family, holiday meal.

And thus: Food—The Saga.

When I'd met Boyd, about a year before that Christmas, I'd been a patient at Horizon House, a residential eating disorders program. Horizon House was a creaky heritage home near the ocean, and the entire structure whistled and shook on windy nights. My cohort included eleven women and exactly one man (a long-haul truck driver) plus a rotating staff of counsellors and dieticians. Our days were spent at the hospital, learning to separate food from feelings, and our evenings were spent at Horizon, the post-dinner group therapy mandatory lest anyone feel the need to regurgitate into the bushes. Instead of Horizon House scaring Boyd off, it fascinated him.

Horizon patients were allowed to invite guests, once vetted, to dinner, and Boyd had been my guest on one of my last nights in the program. I briefed him on what to expect: a house full of women, one man; bodies ranging from the painfully skeletal to the deceptively average (mine somewhere in the middle); and a buffet-style meal, with measuring cups and scales on hand to assuage the stress of 'eyeballing' portions. At Horizon, a plate of food transformed into a math equation. Participants were assigned personalized food plans, and it was not uncommon for meals to begin with a cacophony of counting. "Okay, two starches, three proteins, two vegetables . . ."

On the night Boyd came for dinner, Katy—the Horizon counsellor who most resembled a prison guard—stood beside the food table watching us prep our plates and making sure that no one skimped. "You don't have to measure, Boyd. Unless you want to."

Boyd, the metabolic wonder, piled his plate high and, as he gleefully ate everything, the rest of the table eyed his wiry body with suspicion. What's his secret? Purging?

My eating issues, like most, were symptoms of much deeper problems, ones that six months at Horizon barely managed to poke. But I wanted to believe that, like a bee at a picnic, the problems, if ignored, would just fly away on their own.

Post-Horizon, I joked with Boyd about my continued attachment to measuring ("Have you seen the half-cup? These grapes ain't gonna measure themselves"), about my hyper-vigilance with ingredients ("Did you put cheese in this? That fundamentally complicates things"). I presented my food quirks as being on par with the 'kooky' things an indie-film character might do, like wearing 3D glasses as a fashion statement. I wasn't looking forward to the day Boyd realized he had mistaken 'nihilistically self-destructive' for 'cute and neurotic.' And I didn't want Christmas to be that day.

Matty and I finished our smokes, and when we came inside, Penelope and Pete were there, chatting with Randa in the kitchen. Penelope was tall, like the brothers, and looked like she'd be good at shot put, like she could easily shot put me right over the roof. She radiated vigour and good cheer, her cheeks flushed and her hair shiny. I felt instantly more Wednesday Adams than usual: pale, small, intense. Deviant.

"Hi, I'm Penelope. And this is Pete . . . my little husband!" Pete was short, closer to my height, and delicately boned. Penelope started patting him on the head, and Pete held his smooth hands before him like paws and panted. Longer than was necessary to convey that he was pretending to be a canine with his owner.

Paging Dr. Freud.

"Dinner's ready!" Randa pulled a tray out of the oven, wearing oversized oven mitts that made her look like she had the hands of a sports mascot. "Boyd? Where are you?"

Boyd appeared at the kitchen door, scissors and scotch tape in hand. "I was just wrapping your present, Mom."

Boyd was big on homemade gifts—had inherited the crafting gene from Randa—and, last week, he'd brought home a jumbo Tonka truck from the Salvation Army.

I said, "You bought your mom a secondhand toy truck for Christmas?"

"Yeah. I thought it'd look cool in her garden, like a lawn ornament. Wanna help me paint it?"

I should've said no, since the one time I'd tried painting my toenails my feet ended up looking like they had gangrene.

"Sure."

We laid out newspaper on the hardwood floor of our apartment, put on The Pixies for artistic inspiration. And the section of the truck that Boyd painted, at least, turned out perfect. I wanted to make amends before Randa saw the truck's nether regions.

"Can I help with dinner?"

I ferried plates from kitchen to table as frantic Horizon-like calculations swirled through my brain. *Mashed potatoes! Shit, shit, shit. One spoonful = one starch, one dairy, one fat? Turkey. Same as chicken. Both birds. One serving = palm-sized. But is that my palm? Boyd's palm? A baby's palm?*

I decided to count each glass of wine as one fruit serving and was confident that, once enough 'fruit' had been ingested, nothing that came over the next twenty-four hours would even matter.

Randa had set the dining room table with a few festive flourishes. She'd placed a holly plant as a centrepiece, and during dinner I tried to hide, strategically, behind this plant. I answered a few perfunctory questions—*What sort of work do you do, Jaki?* I'm an ESL tutor. *Do you like it?* I do—then mostly listened as the family reminisced about Christmases past.

Remember when Matty's sled went down the hill without him and crashed into a tree and split in two? Remember when we brought the Christmas tree home and Pebbles wouldn't stop barking at it? RIP Pebbles.

I ate what was on my plate, too wound up to taste much, and genuinely loved listening to the family stories. Boyd made sure to include me with his little asides—*You'd have loved Pebbles. She was a schnauzer. The ones with the drooly beards?* —and Randa beamed, surrounded by her children. Penelope laughed her booming laugh, while Pete tended to cover his mouth when laughing, like a geisha. Even Matty grinned a bit. Food, wine, stories, comfort. I was keen on at least three of the core Christmas elements.

No amount of wine, though, could eradicate that mysterious 'thing' that made me feel, always and forever, separate. And whenever alienation made its presence known—a pressure in my sternum, a thieving of any joy—I redirected my attention to the holly plant. *And what is it that you remember, Holly? The day you got your berries, or the day you got your spikes?*

I suppose I could have shared a story about when I was

eleven and my parents took me to Israel. We did all the touristy things: climbed Mount Masada, floated in the Dead Sea, rode buggies through the Negev desert. And when we got to Jerusalem, we set aside a full day to explore the Old City and each of its four quarters (Muslim, Christian, Jewish, Armenian).

Loitering around the entrance was a gaggle of tour guides, smoking and gossiping and waiting to pounce. The three of us—Mom, Dad and I—were clearly tourists, with our cameras and walking shoes and maps for consulting.

An olive-skinned man of nebulous origins—Jewish, Muslim, Christian, Armenian or none of the above—broke from the pack and claimed us before anyone else could. He had leathery, sun-weathered skin, which made him look like he knew what he was talking about. He and my dad joked around a bit, haggled over the price, and then we three became four.

The guide spoke a mile a minute, and the first three-quarters felt rushed. We did get to step inside the Dome of the Rock, leaving our shoes at the entrance, and see the mosaicked underside of its spherical bronze roof. We touched the Wailing Wall, left notes with our wishes written on them ("World peace and a Nintendo Playstation") in the cracks between limestone blocks.

But our tour guide slowed down significantly when we

reached the Christian section, lingering with reverence at each stop along the Via Dolorosa. Even his speech slowed down.

"This . . . is where Pilate condemned Jesus."

"This . . . is where Jesus stumbled under the weight of the cross."

"This . . . is where Mary met Jesus for the last time."

My eleven-year-old self was enthralled. The story of Jesus, as relayed by the guide, was epic, like an Indiana Jones film, only sad. It had heroes and villains, it had high moral stakes, it had exotic and dusty locales. It had gravitas.

My parents, though polite, were less riveted. I noticed my dad kept checking his watch.

The tour ended at the fourteenth station of the Via Dolorosa, where Jesus had been laid in the tomb. We stood before a baroque and cavernous shrine, surrounded by oversized candles and patterned floors, and our tour guide took a moment to absorb his surroundings. He made the sign of the cross.

"Do you have any questions?"

I tentatively put up my hand.

"Who's Jesus?"

My parents laughed, but the guide looked stunned. "Jesus, my dear, was our Lord and Saviour! He died for our sins."

I was in Grade 5, so my 'sins' consisted of prank calling

strangers from the phone book and stealing small change from my dad's coin jar. If Jesus had died for those, maybe I owed it to the guy to aim a bit higher on the sin ladder going forward.

On the plane ride back to Vancouver, Dad asked me what part of the trip I'd liked best. I didn't hesitate. "Jesus. Definitely Jesus."

Even with limited information, something told me that Jesus, regardless of how many people surrounded him, had moved through his life alone.

And I got that. I really, really got that.

On Christmas Day, after the presents ("Oh! A truck?") and a waffle brunch—during which I relaxed a bit, conjured a former self able to enjoy the blueberry sauce and the whipped cream—Boyd and I went for a walk. The city was deserted, all the businesses closed, but I liked how unpretentious it was. I imagined one of everything: one bakery, one general store, one hitching post, one saloon, even though Campbell River was a real-life city, not a Western movie set.

"I don't think Matty likes me. Has he said anything?"

"Well, Matty doesn't like most people. But yeah, he did mention that he thinks you're a bit fake."

Ouch. Boyd could be blunt. He once told me that I danced like a bored housewife who hadn't been out of the house for a year. But . . . fake? I wanted to believe that I wasn't so much 'fake' as trying to hide the parts of myself that I deemed unpalatable.

"I guess I'll be sure to give him air-kisses when we get back. 'Mwah, mwah . . . Matty darling, you look faaaaahbluous!'"

It was easier to make Boyd laugh than to get into anything serious. The close quarters of Randa's house meant that, at least for this weekend, my avoidance of physical intimacy wasn't at issue, something I couldn't say for our life in Vancouver. There, whenever I managed to end the day fully clothed and without having had to confront my sex-related fears and confusions, I felt like I'd gotten away with something. On second thought, maybe we could stay forever? "What's next on the agenda?"

"*Benny and Joon*. It's a Christmas tradition."

"The movie with Johnny Depp?"

"Yup."

"Huh. Never seen it."

I had no clue what *Benny and Joon* was about, but assumed it had some sort of Christmas theme. It seemed an obscure choice for a family favourite, but since I had once, accidentally, taken my mom to hard-core gay porn at a film festival, who was I to judge?

We got back to everyone snuggled in the TV room.

Penelope and Pete were wearing matching flannel pyjamas with a candy cane design, Pete curled up tight on Penelope's lap. Randa was on the lazy-boy, working on her knitting, and Matty was manspreading on the couch, TV remote pointed at the screen and left foot tapping. "Everyone ready? I'm pressing play."

I tried to think of something not-fake-sounding to say, but it was easier to just find a place to sit.

Benny and Joon is a misnomer, since the film is actually a love story between Joon (Mary Stuart Masterson)—an angelic blond afflicted by an 'adorable' mental illness that caused her to do 'adorable' things like wear a scuba mask while she directs traffic—and someone named Sam (Johnny Depp)—an equally angelic 'eccentric' who dresses like Buster Keaton and makes grilled cheese sandwiches with a clothes iron.

The whole endeavour was cloyingly twee, my least favourite genre, but I seemed to be the only one hate-watching. So I kept my mouth shut, in spite of having plenty to say on the subject. For a film about mental illness, *Benny and Joon* barely touched on the significant ways mental illness wreaked havoc on one's life and on the lives of those around them. The only scene that came near (Joon hearing voices and having a meltdown on public transit) was brief and promptly abandoned for more whimsy

(Depp using physical comedy to try and bust Joon out of a psychiatric facility).

By the end of the film, I was glaring at the DVD player with the intensity of Carrie at her prom, willing it to combust.

"I love that movie more and more each time I watch it! Little husband, would you pull a Johnny and fake insanity to break me out of the loony bin?"

Pete winked at the rest of us. "Nah. I would leave you in there for a while. Let the doctors work their magic."

Hahahahahahahaha.

In Grade 9, at age fourteen, I changed schools. I convinced my parents to send me to York House Secondary, an all-girls private school, since some girls I'd befriended at summer camp went there. York House was hidden behind a perfectly manicured wall of hedges, and my Jewish life, left behind, would never find me there.

The school's landscaping may have been pristine but the student body was anything but. Whoever had come up with the plaid kilt/knee sock combo had to have been a fan of Nabokov. Take a bunch of teenage girls, stick them in tiny wrap-around skirts held together with safety pins, and set them loose in the world. What could possibly go wrong?

Rather than judge you for what you did do, the York

House girls—the Yorkies—judged you for what you didn't do. Smoking, drinking, getting high, having sex and shoplifting were pretty much requisites to run with the glossy-haired crew. "Got me some last night," would brag one glossy girl to another, her smile mischievous, her braces glinting. In this milieu, I was an amateur, a late-bloomer. And I wanted in.

"We're going to steal bras from La Vie en Rose after school. Wanna come?" *Yup.*

"My parents are going away this weekend and we're going to raid their liquor cabinet. Wanna come?" *Yup.*

"We're meeting the boys at the reservoir tonight. Wanna come?" *Yup.*

Boys, even at an all-girls school, were top-of-the-pyramid, numero uno, and one certain crew was valued above all others. The boys in this crew were older, rougher, wilder, meaner, always driving around in muscle cars that stank of weed. Securing their attention was a sacred task for the Yorkies, on par with fixing the hole in the Ozone, still a concern in the nineties.

"Do not, under any circumstances, mention having a curfew or they'll think we're losers," instructed our queen bee, Talia. "If you have to go home, just say you're going to meet your college boyfriend."

No curfew. College boyfriend. A newbie, my spot in the group still tenuous, I catalogued Talia's every word.

The reservoir—the 'res'—was a clearing in the middle of some parkland and a place for teens to drink and hang out after dark. There were no lights there, no benches. Just a slab of concrete surrounded by trees and lit by the moon on clear enough nights. Exchanges like these were a given at the res:

"Joey . . . you got any gas money?"

"No way, man. You never paid me back from last time."

"Screw you, Joey! Don't be a Jew!"

"Cosmo . . . gimme a smoke."

"You can finish this one."

"Aw, don't Jew me man! I want a fresh one."

"Holy shit. Mike got totally Jew'd at the pawn shop today!"

I don't think the boys—Joey, Cosmo, Mike, et al—knew I was Jewish, but even if they had I doubt it would've changed anything. And instead of making me feel outraged, these remarks made me feel ashamed. Ashamed of being Jewish, ashamed of my silence and the silence of my new friends. Ashamed of being, for the first time in my life, one of the only Jews around.

York House was supposed to be non-denominational, welcoming to all, but at Christmastime denomination crept in. In December each year, the entire student body gathered at a local church for the holiday concert, a singalong with

piano accompaniment. And year after year, the song list read
something like this:

In the Bleak Mid-Winter

O Come All Ye Faithful

Silent Night

Once in Royal David's City

The First Noël

God Rest Ye Merry Gentlemen

Away in a Manger

Do You Hear What I Hear?

Jingle Bells

   [Intermission]

Dreidel, Dreidel, Dreidel

   [Refreshments served]

On Boxing Day morning, we were packed and ready to go.
Matty was driving us to Vancouver this time, so I wouldn't
have the chance to debrief with Boyd on the trip, but that
was okay. At least I'd have a free cigarette to smoke on the
ferry deck, sheltered in a corner from the overwhelming
wind.

The weekend had gone, objectively, well, had even been
on the uneventful side. We ate, we drank, we walked, we
lounged. As a homebody, I was actually uniquely suited to
a secular Christmas, but I beat myself up regardless: too

aloof, too inscrutable. I had succeeded in being the most unobtrusive houseguest possible, leaving no discernable trace of having been there at all. They may have found me disconcerting, but they couldn't accuse me of being messy. Like a master of illusion, I knew how to erase myself while still being, physically, in the room.

"Thanks for having me, Randa! So great to meet you, Penelope and Pete!"

"You too, Jaki. Safe travels."

We hugged goodbye at the doorway, more comfortable in each other's presence than we'd been all weekend. I think we all knew that I was a one-and-done; that I wouldn't be back next Christmas or the one after that. That Boyd and I wouldn't last long, and that next year he'd bring someone more relatable, more accessible, less shuttered. Someone who knew, and had always known, the difference between macramé and crochet. Maybe someone with their own Christmas tales to contribute.

And I'd still be me. Wandering the earth. Searching.

"We'd better get going." Matty worked as an electrician, had clients lined up for the next day. "Ferry lines might be bad."

Pulled Pork, Brisket, Polish Ham

OLA SZCZECINSKA

I was in the midst of a several-months'-long nervous break-down when a Vancouver police officer pulled me over for my illegal use of a handheld communication device. I hadn't noticed him ride up alongside me on his bicycle, because I'd been completely focused on rehearsing the spiel I was going to give that day at Money Mart. The idea was: step one, convince Money Mart to lend me the money; step two, get sandwich; step three, vacate my temporary home for the night (i.e. my Toyota) for a motel room; step four, shower until the last several months had thoroughly washed off.

My plan was bulletproof, and I fully expected it to go off without a hitch. There was just a slight wrinkle with that police officer on a bicycle. But I'll explain in a minute.

It started a day earlier. The leaves had all fallen, and I was lurking the Vancouver streets again in my Toyota, hunting for a good parking lot to sleep in that night. I sent a text message: *Hi Nawal! Remember me? We met at Vipassana in January. I was wondering, could I sleep on your couch?*

I'd met Nawal at a silent retreat in Merritt, British Columbia. I'd fled there in a state of grief. I had lost first my home—after my landlord decided to cash in on the inflated housing market—then my partner of eight years, who had four years earlier insisted we move together from Toronto to Vancouver, and then met a woman at a tree planting camp and declared our relationship over. I didn't know where to go or what to do when he suddenly left, or even who I was.

"Everchanging, everchanging," the teacher at the Vipassana retreat had said. *Anicca. Transience. Impermanence.* "Dukkha," he said. "Attachment is the cause of all suffering."

I sat cross-legged with my eyes closed in a dimly lit hall and thought, Exactly, exactly.

I was feeling better, stronger and clearer in my mind. Maybe I could do this, I thought. Maybe I could start over again. Things got worse right after that.

My dad died suddenly, the day after I finished the retreat, and I plunged into a reawakened state of shock and grief. He had finally stopped drinking three weeks earlier, but it was too late. Once again, I did not know how to be or what to do.

I flew to Toronto the next day, accompanied by a sorrow I'd never felt before.

We cremated my father shortly after, then buried him later near Algonquin Park, not far from a river he'd loved to fish, where we'd spent nearly every summer camping.

One thing I recall is my mom asking me to go with her to Ikea right after my dad was cremated. At the time I thought we could take a contemplative stroll by the lake afterwards, or head home and have tea while travelling quietly through our memories of him, so fresh and strong at that time. But my mom had practically begged me. Pleading is something she'd never done before.

"Please," she whispered.

We wandered around with the other zombies and their screaming zombie children through the endless corridors of gleaming white bed frames and woven tapestries with accessible prints. We went to thrift stores as well that week to donate his belongings; we looked through photographs, cancelled his cell plan and car payments.

Then I returned to Vancouver.

I didn't really know where else to go. It felt like the universe was wide open, like I could go anywhere, be anyone, and I couldn't decide: should I live in BC? The Yukon? Rome or Argentina? Did I think it would be fun to check out Antarctica for a while, maybe hang out with the scientists? Yes, I did think that would be fun. These all felt like equally reasonable options at the time. But really the only thing they had in common was my lack of connection to any of them, and that was exciting. I wanted to go someplace new, start over.

✳

Returning to Toronto had felt like failing, an admission that I hadn't succeeded in building a life for myself like I'd set out to do when we'd moved west in 2014. Plus, I still had a shared storage unit with my ex, filled with our old life: Ikea lamps, Le Creuset pots, plates and towels from The Bay. I imagined I would want some of that stuff for my new home, wherever that would be. It was so hard to decide, I was scared of choosing poorly and procrastinated in deciding. It was like living the life of an indecisive existentialist, which sounds terrible, and it was. All the places I thought of sounded equally great and not-great, but I knew no one could choose for me, so I ended up failing to choose at all.

I don't really remember the flight back. I had a small amount of my father's ashes in a keepsake with me—a black heart made of porcelain with butterflies painted on it, which my mother and sister also got—but I don't remember if I told the airport security I had the ashes on my person, which by law you are required to do, or if I buried them deep in my suitcase and kept the secret to myself, so that I wouldn't have to speak of my father's death. I had real anxiety about an agent confiscating them. Probably because I'd failed to acquire the official documentation to travel with remains; there was no way I could have done the paperwork. And I didn't care—I was taking my dad with me; it didn't matter what anyone else said.

Upon returning to Vancouver I was immediately robbed. I had just picked my car up from where I'd left it at a former neighbour's house, transferred my belongings into it from the storage unit, and set out towards a cheap sublet I'd seen an ad for—and had earlier paid a deposit for—in the Yukon. So I wasn't really returning to Vancouver. I had decided to try living up north a while, see if maybe I liked it, maybe it was where I belonged. I had an idea that there were other misfits up there like me, people attracted to vast empty spaces, open roads, uncharted paths and oblivion around every corner. So I loaded my car with all the stuff that I cared about.

But fifteen minutes later, after I'd run into a store for some last-minute Yukon essentials, shards of glass lay below my passenger window and everything inside my car was gone, including the small keepsake of my father. I was devastated, shocked. For hours I reeled with disbelief, unable to leave the parking spot long after the police officers—and the sun—had gone.

But finally what could I do? Annica, dukkha; everything was gone. I had to let go.

I spent the following day recklessly credit-carding some of my life back: jeans, shoes, a laptop, socks and underwear and a toothbrush, lipstick, and lingerie. The next day, I set

*

back out on the road. The sun was high in a beautiful winter sky, and I assured myself that everything would be alright.

The next day I crashed my car.

I slid across a patch of black ice on the highway, and I spun and spun and spun and spun, my car skating in large circles across the road.

I smashed many times against a snowbank, my car banging and crashing as my bones sustained each impact, and I was certain that death was imminent. Then, just like that, everything stopped. I sat in my car stunned, shaking and pinching myself to see if I was still alive. I couldn't believe I was.

I was towed to the closest town, an hour away, paid for by my credit card.

My car was totalled, my insurance didn't cover any of it, and I was now too injured to return to my bush camp job that spring. I paid for a flight—by credit card—and flew with my few newly acquired belongings to my temporary sublet. When I arrived, I crawled underneath the duvet and for many days I did not get up.

I decided to stop trying, then, for at least a little while.

My friends sent their condolences, and called, and my mother—in her own bereaved state—did check in on me frequently, and I on her.

But in the end, I was thirty-nine years old, on my own,

and no one could help me minute by minute as I struggled onward, like an inchworm, through my pain.

I hoped my back injuries would heal in time for a cooking contract I had lined up—still seven months away—and enlisted a physiotherapist paid for by my credit card. In the meantime I relied on the modest inheritance I received from my father—$10,000—to pay for rent, food, and a new used car. Those funds dried up quickly, my sublet ended, and I began to drift from gig to gig and to sleep in one non-place after another.

I struggled with a monster-sized wave of depression. I became anxious and stressed, easily falling into weeping spells over small daily obstacles. I didn't know where home was, and I was unsure there was any point in trying to build one anyhow on such unstable ground that was life on earth.

But the message from the Vipassana centre—everchanging, everchanging—helped me to cope with all that. Life, I began to say to friends and to random people, was all about getting better at letting go.

By December, when I texted Nawal if I could stay the night, I had adapted to my wreck of a life. I was living sometimes here, sometimes there, and sometimes nowhere at all, which at this point was mostly Vancouver. I was too ashamed to ask my mom or friends for help, too ashamed to have anyone I cared about see me looking like a failure, so I stayed with random acquaintances—like Nawal—when I could, or in my car when I couldn't. At age thirty-nine, I'd suddenly become a vagabond, equipped with a story to justify it.

Nawal's reply to my text message had been No. Well, she was out of town, she said. She was sorry and hoped I was well. But then, a few hours later, as I prowled the city for a parking lot to sleep in, she texted me once more.

I just remembered. My condo has remote access. I can buzz you in! Do you still need a place to stay?

Yes, I did, I said.

She sent me her address, said I could park for free in the underground, and that I should drink her tea and use her bath salts. I thanked her profusely, promised her I would be gone the next morning for the flight I had booked to Toronto—it was almost Christmas, and I was going home.

Her place was real nice, a one-bedroom downtown with a den and a bay window overlooking columns of glittering skyscrapers, the ocean, a couple of distant suspension bridges and the mountains beyond. Inside was clean, quiet, and cozy. Rugs covered the floor and positive messages hung or rested in frames all over—Love is God, Namaste, Love Grows Karma—from which I mostly shielded my eyes. After everything that had happened that year, I was living in a sort of open terror of the universe, and I found her messages about God and karma deeply disturbing and offensive.

I sat down on her loveseat, pulled out a bag of trail mix from my bag—my dinner that night—and crunched on some seeds as I contemplated one of Nawal's lengthier messages, which extolled the virtues of surrendering and of accepting our true state of impermanence. I dug around for some raisins in my Ziploc bag and I thought: exactly. Then I had a nice bath.

I slept like a baby in her bed, drifted into a deep, comatose sleep to the soothing sounds of her gurgling pink lava lamp. I woke up feeling regenerated and filled with hope. I tore out of bed.

Outside it was sunny for the first time in many days, and warm light cascaded through the window and I thought: everything is going to be okay.

My mother had already sent me a text that morning, from Toronto, asking me if I wanted a pick-up from the airport.

It's okay, Mom, I replied. I'll just hop on the bus.

She messaged me back right away: she had bought me some organic coffee cream and whole milk from the Metro. Did I want something else?

No. Thanks, Mom, I said. That is great.

She messaged me right back: Was I sure? She was going to the Polish deli shortly and could get me some Polish ham.

It was the thing my mother lovingly stuck into my lunch buns all through elementary and high school, nearly every day. I liked the ham as a kid, the ham was good. It had the added bonus of not smelling like kielbasa, which, when stuck between a bun and pulled out a few hours later at lunchtime, had a way of surrounding me and all the children next to me for the whole hour—like a whoopie cushion—reminding everyone of my Polishness and their Italianness, which, according to them, was superior.

I know they felt this way because they said so verbatim. ('Italians make the best shoes. Italians make the best cheese. Italians make the best clothes. What do Polish people do, anything?' My answer, 'kielbasa,' was not super exciting to them for some reason). But my whole family loved the ham, loved it. It was definitely on the weekly shopping list my mother wrote for my father before he shuttled us away in the family Dodge Spirit for a day of Polish classes and Polish girl scouts, while he shopped for things like eggs, cheese, and ham and Polish newspapers. It wasn't until I moved out at age twenty-one and failed to buy ham for a few years that I realized—upon eating it again at my parents' place—just how great and special Polish ham really was. I don't actually ever buy Polish ham these days—cold cuts give you cancer—and my mom no longer buys it either—for the same reason. But it's one of the first things we buy when we get together over the holidays. I think it reminds us both of what it used to be when we were a family and ham was in the fridge because my father, who was still around, had put it there.

I messaged her back; I told her I'd take the ham. I have to run now mom, I wrote. Got to catch my flight!

I slipped my phone into my coat pocket when it promptly rang.

It was my mother. I picked up. "I gotta go, Mom!" I said.

"Your flight's tomorrow," she blurted out.

"What?"

"It's tomorrow. Where are you?"

I had forwarded my mother the itinerary of my flight a couple months earlier, after I'd booked it online. This was something I began doing to prevent her from compulsively asking me what day my flight was arriving which, in her defence, she only ever did because I compulsively answered: "I have no idea."

"I'm at a friend's house," I said.

"Can you stay there again tonight?"

"Of course I can," I lied. I told her I'd call her back.

I stared straight ahead through the window onto Nawal's balcony, walked up to it, slid open the door and looked down a moment, considered my options. Then it hit me: Money Mart! What a great idea, I thought.

I closed the balcony door and began scurrying

purposefully around in her condo, feeling really good about myself. Or, rather, I began feeling really good, but not really about myself. More like: mixed feelings. Specifically 'terrible' mixed with 'self-loathing' and 'shame.' I'd never gone to Money Mart before, and my sense was that it was, I don't know, pathetic.

But that's neither here nor there: I was going to Money Mart.

I wrote Nawal a thank-you note, promised myself to send her a gift when I was back in the black then zoomed down the elevator and got into my car. It had fleece blankets in the backseat, coffee cups on the floor and it smelled weird, like someone had been living there. Well, there had been, I realized: me. I thought, I really need to change here. I can't do this anymore. I need a whole other life. Maybe as soon as is possible, I'm not sure. I pulled out of the garage and suddenly felt a jolt of explosive joy as I realized that after I got my money from Money Mart, I could very easily go get a sandwich. I became very excited about this and wondered what I should get. I was thinking pulled pork, but I also wanted beef brisket. I was so torn.

The problem with a brisket sandwich—no matter how tasty it is—is that it is just not a cheap sandwich. Just because I was about to secure a loan from Money Mart didn't mean I should suddenly go crazy and buy things like tender beef subs and Ferraris. I was still me, still just a woman living in her Toyota, and the humble pulled pork would do me just fine. Right? Maybe it depended ultimately on what I came across first, a brisket or a pulled pork, because there were arguments on both sides. It really wasn't so easy to decide, when you stopped to think about it.

There were people in suits marching along the sidewalks, most of them either talking on their phones or staring down at them and I wondered, as I slowly turned onto the main avenue, how people became the way they were. How did one become the kind of person who walked every Monday through Friday to an office in order to pay for things like condos and Nikes? I was around the same age as many of these walkers, I observed: forty-ish. But here I was living in my car, rehearsing a presentation for an employee at Money Mart, while these people here urgently spoke into their phones no doubt to other people who also walked briskly and with purpose down some other sidewalk somewhere, people with clean hair, who had almost certainly eaten a date-cashew bar on their way out some nice-looking door. These people smelled like Irish Spring.

How did they become that way and me this other way, smelling like an old sleeping bag? I wondered whether it was something you were born with, or a choice, or an environment thing, and I wondered if there was a scientific consensus on this presently. I would have to check this on Wikipedia while I ate my sandwich. I was wondering all this because I wanted not to be the way I was anymore, and wondered if this was something that was even on the table for me. Or, if not, if I should just focus on getting myself a better blanket for my car, as that would've in this case been the better use of my energy. It's not that I wanted to be like these psychos, I thought, just that on a scale of Toyota-home to downtown condo, it would be better not to be on the Toyota end of things. I guess I was just thinking that a home might be nice, and—at age thirty-nine—maybe even a family inside of one.

I put a pin in that thought for a moment, as I suddenly remembered that I'd soon be eating a sandwich. I couldn't wait. Of all the possible sandwich options I most wanted to see for myself, the pulled pork kept stealing the show. Of course it was possible Money Mart would deny me access and crush my big dream for the day. In which case I would not cry. Not in front of the gatekeeper, anyway. I would cry at home, in my car. Maybe find someplace nice to park.

I rolled slowly towards a red light some fifty feet away and mentally reviewed the details I'd need to nail in order to ensure the best possible outcome here. At the same time, I reached for my phone and typed in the address. Then I heard a knock on the window.

I swung my head and was momentarily disoriented by two very round blue eyes and a large, shockingly bright yellow moving object filling my entire passenger window, before it all at once crystallized into a hi-vis vest being worn by a police officer on a bicycle, looking at me.

I yelped and threw my phone as though it was a dead rat, but it was too late.

"Pull over," he said.

I did.

I rolled down the one window that was working at the moment, which, happily, was the one right in front of him. "Hello," I said, brightly, after he'd leaned right in. We glanced down at my phone as it lay quiet and innocent on the passenger seat next to me. There was a moment of silence as we both considered it, then I looked back up at him and tried once again to smile.

He asked me for my documents.

Here's the thing. In June I had bought, by complete mistake, a stolen vehicle from a man in Alberta, online. It's a long story. I did get rid of it. But not before first embarking on a desperate stint of frenetic illegal activity in an effort to launder the deal, including forging some insurance papers and registration forms, and these are now what I handed over.

He took a few moments, glanced from the outside of my

car to my papers then to me again and said, "Do you own this vehicle?" The question startled me. I told him that yes I did, but then for a moment I became very worried. Was this my vehicle? It had been quite a year, a bit of a blur, not least because of a certain amount of cabernet that had been drunk. And/or different pills swallowed. Nothing crazy, I'm talking just some ketamine here or there or some Percocets maybe. Large doses of Nyquil in a pinch. I'd actually forgotten all about the previous car, so much had happened since I'd picked it up three months earlier, in the middle of the night in Calgary, from a parking lot, where the guy had told me to get it. "Doors unlocked, keys in glove compartment," he'd said, in an email. "Sounds good!" I'd replied.

"Says here you own a black Toyota Rav4," the officer said. "This one's white."

I yelped once more. "Those are the wrong papers," I blurted out, as I tried to rip the fraudulent registration from his hands. He kindly let me, but he didn't take his eyes off of me, peered at me keenly, with real interest as I rummaged around through my wreck. He then took a good look around my car, his eyes scanning everything as if trying to pull out more of my story, roaming over the blankets, pillows, take-out bags and rumpled clothing, looked me directly in the eyes as I smoothed out the real documents for him, and said, "Are you currently living in your car, ma'am?"

The question hit me like a cannonball; I froze. I looked at him, speechless. It wasn't really the question of whether I was living in my car that hurt—which it did, because I was, and being found out had a way of making me feel bad about it—but actually it was the 'ma'am' that had really done it. At age thirty-nine, a couple months away from forty, the ma'am signified my entrance into a category of humans I had never belonged to before: not-young women. I was now a not-young woman. Forever. Progressively. And the officer, unknowingly, had just made it official with the word ma'am, instead of 'miss.'

I reeled in horror. Ma'am? Ma'am? a floating voice in my head said. I immediately realized this meant only one thing: it was not okay for me to be living in my car anymore. I was too old for that now. Living in a car was tolerated if you were young, because, well, maybe you were just taking a bit of extra time, like: hey, life is hard and confusing. Take a couple more years, why not? That was not the case for a ma'am. For a ma'am it was only one thing: failure.

I burst into tears. I didn't want to cry in front of the police officer, or the downtown passers-by, but that was just too bad. A dam in me had burst and I couldn't stop. It was not great timing, but there it was—sorrow and despair and frustration pouring all out of me, Starbucks cups and rumpled clothing everywhere. So be it. "Yes," I whispered. "I'm sorry."

The officer regarded me with a mix of pity and concern in his eyes, and said he'd be right back.

I leaned my head against the steering wheel and cried while I waited for him to return. It felt nice to do that. Relaxing. I dug around for an old take-out napkin, found one on the floor and blew my nose into it. People walked by and stared at me, phones pressed to their ears, probably speaking to their loved ones and I wondered: why on earth was I living in my car?

Who knows how people become who they are. How they manage to buy condos, and wash their hair at least once a week. That beats me. But as I sat in my car waiting for the officer to return with a ticket I couldn't pay for, I realized none of that mattered. It was not a question of any of that; it was merely a question of falling. Or rather, of landing. It was a question of how long I'd continue to let myself fall, how much longer I'd let life happen to me, instead of the other way around: make my life happen. And it was a question of how long I would allow the story of surrendering and of letting go—a story that had perhaps served me well, for a moment, as I grappled with so much loss—to shape who I was and who I would become. It was not good enough, anymore, to use karma and surrendering as excuses to do nothing, become nobody, and to remain a passive speck of dust floating upon a cosmic breeze.

One of the last things my dad said to me of any consequence was, "is your life still a mess?" I was in Whitehorse at that time. The inside of my car was a wreck, and I wondered how he could see all that from across the country. I can't remember how I replied to him then, probably some version of denial, sarcasm, anger and tears—my usual brew. In my defence, some months later, my therapist had said, "No, your life is *not* a mess. You just live *differently*." But respectfully I disagreed. Had my dad been around in that moment, as the officer peered into my Toyota, pretty sure he would've said, 'Yup. Still a mess.'

"No ticket today," the officer said. "But," he added, gravely, "but ma'am? If you've fallen on some hard times, you can't afford a ticket."

I sniffed and nodded and blew my nose, put my documents away. I thanked him and promised him I wouldn't use my phone while driving ever again, not even while rolling towards a stop.

He nodded, wished me luck and pedalled away.

I started my car up and pulled back out into the Tuesday morning traffic. I was definitely going to Money Mart, there was no doubt about it. I was also, immediately after, going to get myself that sandwich—nothing would stop me.

And there was no way, come hell or high water, that I would be living in my Toyota-home this time next year.

*

I gripped my steering wheel as I drove away, something in me hardening. It was time to dig my nails in, grab a hold of something, and fight for it. It could be anything. Today I'd settle for a pulled pork sandwich.

Because

TOLU OLORUNTOBA

After Joshua Mensch. Customary memoiristic disclaimers, appeals to poetic license and literary deniability, cop-outs, announcements of possible alteration and embellishment, and advisories regarding absence of relevant professional credentials apply. May contain familial violence and a reference to pregnancy loss.

Introduction: The Anti-Karenina Principle

When you're about to stick the corkscrew into the old, perhaps original wound, it is normal to feel a whirling sensation in your core, a terror before its hurtful pirouette through scabs that had just begun to rest. You may also just be tensing from the whiff of traumas past wafting upward with their strangling clasps, taunting you with their immortality.

These, surely, but in my case also because I am trying to fit a world into an essay, and I remain tentative because my thoughts are, however much I have rehearsed them, inconclusive. Because what is planetary to me may be inconsequential to others. Because I may be adding nothing to a psychosocial discussion that is over forty years long. Because it is hard to write critically yet honestly about living relatives that one has had a fraught relationship with, but who one still wants to maintain some community with.

And importantly: because no one needs to read another essay about how Leo Tolstoy was wrong about unhappy families, because they are unique in their own ways. Because the sorrows of those families follow a pattern it is impossible to unsee, once one has seen their arc. To an aphorism of my medical teachers—*diseases do not read textbooks* (so illnesses may not present the exact way one reads about in the texts)—I rebut: but some families do. Because when Sharon Wegscheider disproved Tolstoy's theory of heterogeneous consanguineous dysfunction with a new theory in 1981, she revealed the hitherto arcane logics and mechanics that animate (all, I'd wager) unhappy families.

Another aphorism from my teachers, a variant of Occam's Razor, is: *if you hear hoofbeats outside, it is more likely to be a horse than a zebra*. Because if a family satisfied the definition criteria for dysfunctional families, and acted accordingly, then that family was likely dysfunctional.

A Little Knowledge is a Dangerous Thing, or, A Cat May Look at a King

In my second year of medical school, I discovered dysfunctional family roles. Because I had long suspected that all was not right with my family and the way I grew up, but

I hadn't the words to describe it until then, a picture began to emerge. Dysfunctional family dynamics may have been described initially to give "alcoholic families" a chance at relational health, but they also describe families with other core dysfunctions (including physical and emotional abuse, neglect, narcissism) or addictions. My family had read, and knew by rote, the book; had been on a darkened stage, delivering an instinctive script. Because from my place backstage, the roles that each family member was cast into, in this play of a violent Narcissus, were spotlit before the darkness.

A vignette might illustrate: I am forced to remember the day I had lost some money I was meant to deliver on the father's behalf. He would hear none of the pleas that I had not stolen the money. Not loving the memory, and the burly uncle he brought to whip me to his satisfaction, I want to forget. Because he had locked my siblings, eight and five, outside the house. Because they had been crying and screaming, trying the front and back doors as they heard my screams. Because when your hands, feet, are bound, you learn something of digging to earth yourself, your bunions echoing each lash on the ground, your praying wrists tamping the terrazzo. I remember it was cold, because I was prone, naked as redacted men in CIA black sites. Because it is a heirloom crystal of compressed humiliation, and confrontation with oblivion. I wish I had at least stolen the money he decided that I had.

Retracing my steps, I later found the money between the front seat of his car and the door that night after I had awoken, although I did not recall going to sleep, only the convulsions of total grief I took to my bed. He said nothing, not even an *oh*, when I handed it to him. I was eleven years old. Anyway, he beat me till I was eighteen, in my first year of university. That last time, I hadn't turned on the generator as quickly as he wanted after the power went out.

But not just the kids got it. No one, not his siblings, employees, or recipients of his road rage, was safe from his punching hand.

Our role was to appease god the father in his rages. Because his role was to not listen, and to smite, he made the evangelical God easier to understand. *Apologize to your father.* Mother as chaplain of a conciliatory religion. *He is waiting for you in his room.*

Whenever I hear a car approaching my townhouse (I am thirty-eight, and two oceans away now) my heart rate and blood pressure rise. Because my body remembers running upstairs as a child whenever the father's car arrived. Because, as you always quoted, "A good man leaves an inheritance for his children's children," and because time is a perpetual *because*, and because things happen because other things happen, thanks for the complex trauma, Dad. My therapists thank you as well. The people that have tried to love me after do not.

You see the pattern, the spiral orbit of bodies around starfire, and are changed. Like the prophets of old, you hope that your transfiguration can change others, but because they are as obstinate as you were in their assigned grooves, they do not always listen. Dysfunctional role-call: caretaker/enabler/martyr; hero; mascot/clown; scapegoat/black sheep; lost child; golden child, parentified child. Hey, we're all here! How did those pesky scientists know the family secret, and more about it than even we did? That roles could change. That cast members could play more than one part, all clustered around the star actor: addict or narcissist. That star actors often misbehave but saying only they are problematic is simplistic and not constructive. Because each member, in their role, plays their part in the dysfunction.

I asked the siblings and mother whether they'd heard of this, and what they thought of it. I don't recall them sharing my enthusiasm for the subject. But the discovery was the beginning of my journey inward and downward.

Ah, the chain-link of traumas and protections that later become maladaptive, which help us pass on the same, or improved, traumas, world without end. Or until someone ends it. I cannot explain myself without explaining the father, but I cannot explain the father without explaining *his* father. Because what do you get in this scenario: a child is born in the dying days of the formal subjugation/protection by the British Empire of vanquished territories they had cobbled into a country forty years before. Because this child is born after, and before, a series of miscarriages and still-births. Because most infants where the child was born did not make it past their first birthday (those for whom it was recorded), and many of those did not make it past their fifth. Because he only knew in retrospect the word—poverty—for what he had been born into. Because he did know the dirt floor of his birth, and the hungers of his boyhood, and the groundnut stall he salvaged morsels from after the trading day. But he made his way into schools and found an aptitude for learning, and broke through the huddle of dead bodies to the other side, bloody and bloodthirsty. Because he had forged the hardness of will he needed in a world that had shut the doors; a violence reciprocal to his environment, or greater; and a self-regard and will to power that preserved his walls in a world that would see him dissolved. Because he needed a narcissistic personality to survive, but after he survived, did not know to put the sword and shield away. Picture that at a dining table. I know this by interpretation and from hundreds of monologues, each several hours long, involving crying and self-pity.

The father's father mostly stayed in his room. He had been a sanitation worker in the university the father would eventually attend as an undergraduate. The father may have avoided his father's garbage route, perhaps out of shame. The father's scholarship funds had been appropriated to raise five siblings and four half-siblings, and because he became the breadwinner of his large family as a very young man, his word became law, even over his parents. And because of the father's orientation toward decisive and implacable action, he perhaps viewed his own father as passive. He may have decided he needed to be the opposite of his father, as sons sometimes do as they begin to style themselves. His ruthless drive took him, on another scholarship, to graduate school in California.

I had resolved to take the beatings, the fear, and what I later recognized to be emotional abuse, until I no longer had to. Because I would get a scholarship and go to university. Because if I did not need his money for sustenance and tuition, I would not need to come home or speak to him again. But the thought of leaving the others as his victims gave me significant pause. And because I received none of the scholarships I had hoped for, I remained the father's financial dependent for the next six years after I got shipped off to medical school as a teenager.

Because people tend to converge during the holidays, I was nineteen when, just before my second Christmas holiday in medical school, I decided to stage an intervention with the father. Because if I wasn't going away, I wanted to at least try to make things better. Because I still wistfully hoped things could be better between us and thought that open dialogue would help us begin the dialogue. So (because I was too chicken to do it face-to-face), I sent him what I've called the Truth and Reconciliation email when he was out of town. I told of how my siblings and I had grown up in an atmosphere of fear and terror. And because I wanted the formal, frosty, fraught relationship we had to improve, I felt the substructure of our family needed some work, for us to get to that future.

Thank you for this interesting email. Let us discuss it when I get back.

Yes! This was it. Better news than I had expected.

Counter-maneuvers, or You Come at the King, You Best Not Miss

But calling out family dysfunction or choosing not to be a part of that cycle often comes at a high cost. So . . . it didn't go well for me. In patriarchal or otherwise oppressive groups, penalty clauses for opting out of the social contract parallel what happens to the black sheep, or identified patient, of dysfunctional families. Excommunication but first, punishment.

When attempts are made to hold abusive perpetrators to account, they may resort to a pattern of response that has been called DARVO (Deny, Attack, Reverse the Roles of Victim and Offender). Such sweet knowledge. Not so helpful in hindsight.

More hindsight: textbooks say what I had was a dysfunctional narcissistic family or authoritarian family with similar but nuanced "rules." I needed this information twenty years ago. Because he came out swinging. Because at the family meeting he called, he distributed printouts of my email. Because he read the charges as I stood before the seated tribunal. Because the others were stunned by the contents because they did not see it coming. Because there were several *Ohshitohshitohshit* and *This is true but how could you say it* beats. The siblings were young teenagers by then. He turned to them and asked them if what I said in the email was true. He asked the mother as well. They later told me they should not have abandoned me since I had been speaking for all of us. But from what I now understand about power imbalances and other dynamics, they could not have agreed that it was a correct representation of the facts. At any rate, only the father spoke freely in that house. Because there was simply no one (up to that point) who had contradicted him so directly. What followed was a four-hour rant in which he accused me of emailing in bad faith, of saying that our substructure was weak to disparage the parents, since they were the substructure (his interpretation). He said he had already called his lawyer and had me removed from the will, etcetera, etcetera.

Apologize to your father. So I apologized for sending the email, not for the contents. Because I was indeed sorry to have learned too late how subject to misinterpretation the written word could be, and how one's emails could be used against them. Because I was tired of the tirade, the denials, the betrayal of it all, and the pins-and-needles in my legs. Because I realized I was not going to win and I really would like to sleep. At the risk of being a Sun Tzu bro, I'll say I had remembered too late what the sage had said: "When you surround an army, leave an outlet free. Do not press a desperate foe too hard."

For someone in the "good offence" school of defensiveness, he of course vehemently rejected any suggestion of wrongdoing. In the morning, he did not address any of the events of the night before, but he did hand me keys to his old Benz (grounded from a bad engine) and said he was giving it to me. He later fixed the car and used it personally, and eventually sold it, but that's another story. My point is the father never apologized to me for anything until I was thirty-six (and then, only in oblique fashion, *for anything* that [he] did).

I could not have known to read *Difficult Conversations*, the 1999 book by Stone, Patton, and Heen, to prepare me for the ultimately failed intervention I would later stage with the father over the holidays, armed with my new knowledge of dysfunction in families. Because in fact, I only knew of and read the book in this year. There are many conflicts that require more than a difficult conversation (however deftly navigated) to solve. Nonetheless, the book says "difficult conversations are almost never about getting the facts right. They are about conflicting perceptions, interpretations, and values . . . they are about what is important." I consider this to be true. Because I'd been arguing with facts to force an admission, and negotiation. Because we did not see the facts in the same way. Because there were complex injuries that needed to be addressed beyond any introduction of the topic. Because knowing that "difficult conversations do not just involve feelings, they are their very core about feelings," I was in over my head. And because at any rate, the family needed a qualified mediator, not a non-emancipated teenager, to guide an extended period of trauma-informed treatment.

You Can Never Go Back, or Christmas Ain't the Same
Of course, it is not fair to say I (or anyone) could have ruined the holidays single-handed. Nonetheless, holidays

*

are especially difficult times for dysfunctional families. A Google search of "holidays with dysfunctional families" yielded 738 million results in 0.48 seconds.

There were many things I did not, or could not have known, but I did know I wanted our family reconciled. Because I wanted an us *sans* despair and stage whispers, perhaps with a non-volcanic father thrown in. Because I wanted a secure and calm (and perhaps even happy at some point) home for all of us. Because I wish we all got more for, and out of, these desires. Because I wish we were all ready when a moment, or several, presented.

In an alternate reality, all these happened. And the country did not crumble under the gravity of decades of juntas. And the thing that had happened that December did not keep me in school for most holidays. And after our cautious climb out of the nest and to university, my siblings and I felt we could, and liked to, go back home. And we held on to our photos with Father Christmas, invariably crying in a nonetheless happy time. And we fondly remembered the newly bought (if previously owned) clothes; chickens being defeathered in boiling water; rice on the stove; Boney M's Christmas album playing from the record player, and the faint but sweet smell of Harmattan dust in the chilly December air. And it took years, but we finally reached a truce. And no one killed that Christmas. And the magic of

Christmas, and Rice and Stew Very Plenty, remained. What if Jesus was not in fact born in December at all? I may have come to question my faith, but I would never doubt the love we would have been able to multiply. And the definition of home would not vanish, it would only have expanded. And the 276 schoolgirls of Chibok, and many others, would have written their final exams and graduated into lives of their own. And we might have lived outside Nigeria, but there was a country we could call ours, that one could return to. And in that country, there was a home that held memory and promise in tension.

Complex PTSD, or other kinds of trauma, can ruin the memory or experience of holidays forever in some cases. As a Nigerian, I harbour national trauma (and shame), and as the child of a dysfunctional family, I have been given other toxic gifts. We have an uneasy peace but better-defined boundaries today; some of us have been in therapy, including those who had been skeptical of it. Because the poles of the dysfunctional set have shifted, but not vanished.

Guess Who's Coming Home for Christmas

In the movies *Edge of Tomorrow: Live Die Repeat* and *Source Code*, and the *Russian Doll* TV series, the protagonist must make choices, within several iterations of a time anomaly, that change the course of a present and/or future. One example of such a time-choice story is holiday-themed: *A Christmas Carol*. What must this protagonist do to secure a different (and improved) future, or at least stave off disaster?

Things are similar now but different. I still do not know what, or if, to do. But I do know the protagonist is not one person, but one family. Because I feel duty-bound to prevent spoilage in each iteration, like the fruit bowls in the first *Russian Doll*. Because if the past is not even past, although relationships can be repaired; and our choices mean things; and it would perhaps be great to have a happy Christmas all together again someday; what can I, or could I, or should I do? (Not to be all, my therapist says, but my therapist says should is often a bad word.) And if we want it but are not moving toward it, will things be better next year?

Contributors

Jennifer Allen studied creative writing at the University of Toronto. A finalist for the Penguin Random House Award for Student Fiction, she lives in South Surrey where she is a member of the Vancouver Writer's Fest and Creative Non-fiction Society Collective.

Joanna Baxter co-founded and co-hosted a quarterly reading event and podcast called Spiel_Vancouver to support local emerging writers. She is currently working on a collection of short stories. Joanna lives with her husband and two teenagers on Vancouver's North Shore.

Jaki Eisman's work can be found in *Room* and *Open Minds Quarterly*. She is currently writing a tragicomic memoir about the challenges, victories, and spiritual opportunities of a life spent dealing with mental illness. She lives in Vancouver with her fluffy cat, Nunu.

Wiley Wei-Chiun Ho is an award-winning author whose short stories and personal essays have appeared in *River Teeth, ROOM, PRISM international, Ricepaper, WordWorks,* and the anthology *Chrysanthemum: Voices of the Taiwanese*

Diaspora. A member of the Asian Canadian Writers' Workshop, she also serves on the boards of the Federation of BC Writers and the North Shore Writers' Association. When dodging her desk, she can be found forest-bathing and tree-hugging.

Joseph Kakwinokanasum is a member of the James Smith Cree Nation who grew up in the Peace region of northern BC, one of seven children raised by a single mother. In 2022, he was named a Rising Star by The Writers' Union of Canada. His debut novel, *My Indian Summer* (Tidewater Press), received the 2023 First Nations Communities Read award and was shortlisted for the ReLit award for fiction.

Jordan Kawchuk has spent his career in the media, producing and writing for TV, radio, and podcasts that include shows like *This Hour Has 22 Minutes* and projects for National Geographic, Discovery, Slack, and The Food Network. He is currently working on a book about his adventures touring the world as a sax player with a boozy swing band.

Sonja Larsen's memoir, *Red Star Tattoo: My Life as a Girl Revolutionary* (Random House Canada), won the 2017 Edna Staebler Non-fiction Award and was shortlisted for The Writers' Trust Non-fiction Award. Her flash non-fiction and short stories have appeared in literary publications in the US, Canada and the UK. She lives in Vancouver, BC.

JJ Lee's debut book, *The Measure of a Man: The Story of a Father, a Son, and a Suit* (McClelland & Stewart) was a finalist for the Hilary Weston, Charles Taylor, Hubert Evans and Governor General's awards for non-fiction. For ten years, he was a contributor, reporter, producer, and host for CBC Radio and now leads a non-fiction workshop at The Writer's Studio at Simon Fraser University.

Tolu Oloruntoba was born in Ibadan, Nigeria, where he studied and practised medicine. He is the author of two collections of poetry: *The Junta of Happenstance* (Palimpsest Press/Anstruther Books), winner of the Canadian Griffin Poetry Prize and Governor General's Literary Award, and *Each One a Furnace* (McClelland & Stewart/Penguin Random House Canada), a Dorothy Livesay Poetry Prize finalist. He lives in Surrey, on Coast Salish lands in western Canada.

Courtney Racicot's short story, "Mirror Images," was long-listed for the 2017 CBC Non-Fiction Award. She lives in northern Ontario with her chocolate Labrador Retriever, Jude, where she is currently writing a novel based on the experiences described in "Aiden."

*

Ola Szczecinska was born in Warsaw, Poland, and moved to Canada with her family in 1984. A graduate of the University of Toronto, her writing has been featured in *Narrative* and *Geist* magazines. She works as a bush-camp cook during the warmer months and lives in Madawaska Valley, Ontario, with her dog, Angel, the rest of the year.

Goran Yerkovich was raised by Croatian immigrant parents on the Canadian Prairies. He has run a top-thirty podcast, is the founder of the The-Inspired.com (read in over 130 countries) and has been published at Fatherly.com. A writer of nostalgic non-fiction, Goran lives in the greater Vancouver area with his wife and two rescue cats, Kimchi and Kauai.